Prairie Town

Critical Perspectives Series
Series Editor: Donaldo Macedo, University of Massachusetts, Boston
A book series dedicated to Paulo Freire

Chomsky on Miseducation
by Noam Chomsky, edited and introduced by Donaldo Macedo

Critical Education in the New Information Age
by Manual Castells, Ramón Flecha, Paulo Freire, Henry A. Giroux,
Donaldo Macedo, and Paul Wills

Critical Ethnicity: Countering the Waves of Identity Politics
edited by Robert H. Tai and Mary L. Kenyatta

Debatable Diversity: Critical Dialogues on Change in American Universities
by Raymond V. Padilla and Miguel Montiel

Imagining Teachers: Rethinking Gender Dynamics in the Classroom
by Gustavo E. Fischman

Immigrant Voices: In Search of Educational Equity
edited by Enrique (Henry) Trueba and Lilia I. Bartolomé

*The Last Good Job in America: Work and Communication in the New Global
Technoculture*
by Stanley Aronowitz

Latinos Unidos: From Cultural Diversity to the Politics of Solidarity
by Enrique (Henry) Trueba

Pedagogy of Freedom: Ethics, Democracy, and Civic Courage
by Paulo Freire

Pedagogy, Symbolic Control, and Identity, Revised Edition
by Basil Bernstein

A Sanctuary of Their Own: Intellectual Refugees in the Academy
by Raphael Sassower

Sharing Words: Theory and Practice of Dialogic Learning
by Ramon Flecha

Ideology Matters (forthcoming)
by Paulo Freire and Donaldo Macedo

Prairie Town

Redefining Rural Life in the Age of Globalization

JACQUELINE EDMONDSON

ROWMAN & LITTLEFIELD PUBLISHERS, INC.
Lanham • Boulder • New York • Toronto • Oxford

ROWMAN & LITTLEFIELD PUBLISHERS, INC.

Published in the United States of America
by Rowman & Littlefield Publishers, Inc.
A wholly owned subsidiary of The Rowman & Littlefield Publishing Group, Inc.
4501 Forbes Boulevard, Suite 200, Lanham, MD 20706
www.rowmanlittlefield.com

P.O. Box 317, Oxford OX2 9RU, UK

British Library Cataloguing in Publication Information Available

Library of Congress Cataloging-in-Publication Data

Edmondson, Jacqueline, 1967–
  Prairie town : redefining rural life in the age of globalization / Jacqueline Edmondson.
    p. cm.—(Critical perspectives series)
  Includes bibliographical references (p.) and index.
  ISBN 0-7425-1941-4 (alk. paper) — ISBN 0-7425-1942-2 (pbk. : alk. paper)
    1. Sociology, Rural—Minnesota. 2. Farm life—Minnesota. 3. Rural poor—
Minnesota. 4. Agricultural industries—Minnesota. 5. Agriculture—Economic aspects—
Minnesota. 6. Agriculture and state—Minnesota. 7. Literacy—Minnesota. 8. Home
economics, Rural—Minnesota. 9. Minnesota—Rural conditions. 10. Minnesota—
Economic conditions. I. Title. II. Series.

HN79.M6E36 2003
307.72'09776—dc21

                                                                            2003043219

Printed in the United States of America

♾™ The paper used in this publication meets the minimum requirements of American
National Standard for Information Sciences—Permanence of Paper for Printed Library
Materials, ANSI/NISO Z39.48-1992.

For Luke, Jacob, and Michael

Contents

Acknowledgments

I must first thank those in "Prairie Town" who were kind enough to share their lives with me. Many teachers, school personnel, and townspeople generously shared their experiences as I worked to make sense of the "rural condition" and literacy's relationship to it. I am thankful to them all. In particular, I must give special thanks to a few individuals who were especially instrumental in this project. Pam Solvie was always willing to help me find additional information, and was ever encouraging to me as she enthusiastically read earlier drafts of this manuscript. Rolly Zeltwanger, David Fluegel, and Philip Drown likewise read earlier drafts of this manuscript, helped me to find additional information as I requested it, and verified the accuracy of different aspects of this work. I also must thank Jason Lina, one of Prairie Town's newspaper reporters, who was kind enough to help me locate people and information. Finally, I thank Pat Nelson and Jessica Nelson, who helped in various times and in different ways as I worked to pull this project together.

I owe my sincerest and most heartfelt thanks to Patrick Shannon. As I corresponded with Pat from Prairie Town, explaining the various town meetings and planning sessions I was involved in, he suggested that I collect interviews and other data. After my data was collected and I was trying to make sense of this work, Pat was always available to listen and to talk with me about this project, to question and to push my thinking, to suggest readings that would help me to make sense of it, and to read drafts of this manuscript. I can never thank him enough.

At Penn State, I must thank Henry Giroux, who helped me to find an editor and publisher for this manuscript and who always was willing to generously share ideas, readings, and his own work with me. Susan Searls Giroux was always available to listen over coffee and make constructive and insightful suggestions. James Dunn in Penn State's College of Agriculture read chapter two and helped me to better understand federal farm policy, farming technology, contracting, and other aspects of agricultural economy. Judy Nastase, always amazing and patient, helped me with the formatting and other technical aspects of this book. Jocelyn McNeel was wonderful help with the indexing.

Donaldo Macedo has been a truly wonderful editor, always encouraging and insightful in his responses to this manuscript. He taught me much about the importance of my own voice in writing, and perhaps more importantly about solidarity. Dean Birkenkamp at Rowman & Littlefield likewise was always supportive and offered constructive and thoughtful suggestions for this project. I must also express thanks to Alison Sullenberger, April Leo, and Kärstin Painter.

Finally, I must thank Michael, Jacob, and Luke. I'll never forget the look on Michael's face as he stepped out of the moving van when we first arrived in Prairie Town, and he (a chef) told me that he wouldn't unpack his cookbooks because we wouldn't be staying for long. In spite of his initial uncertainty, he came to love this community along with me, to read it in a way that recognized the value in it. It was an interesting journey that I'm glad we traveled together, and I look forward to more. As always, Jacob and Luke remain my inspiration and joy, and they continually offer me fresh insights on literacy and life.

Introduction

My husband, Michael, and I, along with our two young children, drove nearly one thousand miles from our home in Pennsylvania toward Prairie Town, Minnesota (pop. 5,067) in order for me to assume a position at the nearby university. The sweltering August sun glared into our eyes as we traveled west on wide, flat roads that would soon become all too familiar over the two years we lived in the Midwest. It was 1998, two years after President Clinton signed the Republican-backed "Freedom to Farm Act" into law. Freedom to Farm was designed to phase out government support of farmers over the seven years of the bill, turning farmers and agricultural production to the invisible hand of the free market. Just months after Clinton signed the bill, farmers in India protested the World Trade Organization's (WTO) multilateral trade agreements and neoliberal[1] policies, demanding India's withdrawal from the WTO. By the time we settled in Prairie Town, more than four hundred peasant farmers and agricultural laborers committed suicide half a world away in Andhara, India in protest of these policies. Poverty, starvation, and desperation due to crop failures, indebtedness, and unequal trade agreements were felt by agricultural workers the world over. Because of the manner in which free trade is institutionalized, struggling countries do not have the material conditions that allow them equal access to international trade markets. For instance, countries like India have difficulty meeting the First World's environmental standards where fruit with bruises or mosquito bites are unacceptable.[2] Just like the French farmers philosopher Pierre Bourdieu interviewed, they are capitalists who cannot "realize their capital."[3] Developing countries do not enter the foreign trade market on a level playing field; in many ways, the odds are already stacked against them. The conditions facing struggling nations leave us to wonder, as Arundhati Roy has asked, whether globalization is "about 'eradication of world poverty,' or [whether it] is a mutated variety of colonialism, remote-controlled and digitally operated?"[4]

Neither Michael nor I had ever lived in a community that was primarily agriculturally based before we settled in Prairie Town. As newcomers, we first noticed the grain elevator looming over the center of town, the tallest structure in sight. It seemed a proud reminder of the agriculture and industry that built the economy in the region. Parallel to Main Street, running past the grain elevator, was the railroad, which connected residents with points unknown since long before the telephone, television, or the Internet. The train remained an important aspect of rural life in Prairie Town, like many communities throughout the Midwest, not just because of its business operations, but also because it marked time in various ways. When the town was officially founded in 1871, it was named after the St. Paul and Pacific Railroad's chief railroad engineer.[5] At that time, the train depot was a hub of activity, bringing people from all over the world to homestead the land, which promised rich soil and a rich life in spite of the isolation and extreme weather conditions. Over the years, the train took Prairie Town's young people off to fight in the world wars, to see the cities, and to live elsewhere. Eventually, passenger train traffic dwindled as automobile travel increased and fewer people came into the community by train, and like many other rural towns, the railroad finally shifted its focus exclusively toward exporting goods. In spite of this shift, the train remained important to local residents, and like many of our neighbors, it didn't take us long to find ourselves marking the segments of our days according to its lonely whistle. By the end of our first winter, we found comfort in its implicit reminder that life was continuing on in spite of the often dangerous winter conditions that kept us isolated and indoors.

During the first harvest after our arrival, we traveled Main Street along the railroad tracks and noticed a large pile of corn accumulating near the grain elevator. We believed the corn was going to be shipped elsewhere, and would soon be transported through the grain elevator to the empty cars that sent goods to Minneapolis, St. Paul, and beyond. However, as the pile grew into a mountain over the next several months, we came to see that it signified something we had never considered, given our roots in suburban America. The corn, which eventually was covered with a patchwork of plastic tarps and old tractor tires to preserve its contents against the harsh winter winds and the geese and ducks that foraged for food, demonstrated a mastery over a particular language of farming and a rural literacy we had never before considered. In other words, the corn pile represented a way in which some in the community were "reading the world," teaching us much about the rural literacies that are the topic of this book. Brazilian educator Paulo Freire, through his extensive literacy work that began with peasants in Brazil, helped us to understand that "reading the world" is essential to literacy, preceding and always informing reading the word.[6] Texts, which in Prairie Town's case would include the corn piles, trains, and the objects, symbols, and things of rural life, are read and interpreted, written and rewritten in an effort to "understand everyday life and the social grammar of the concrete through the larger totalities of history and social context."[7] With Freire's notions of literacy in mind, this book focuses on the histories and contexts that inform the ways in which those living in rural Prairie Town are reading, and consequently writing and rewriting, their world. To begin, a brief description of the context of this work is offered.

Contextualizations

National news coverage of the upper Midwest can run the gamut from the flamboyant to the familiar. In 1998, former professional wrestler and erstwhile radio host Jesse Ventura "shocked the world" as he liked to say, by becoming Minnesota's governor. Ventura promptly followed this accomplishment with a series of media events that ranged from drinking milk at a governor's conference in protest of dairy policies, to criticizing streets constructed by the Irish residents of St. Paul on David Letterman's *Late Show*. Intermingled with the television sound bites of the unpredictable new governor were the more predictable and somber images of Minnesota farmers looking on as crop returns and hog prices plummeted to record lows and family farms went up for auction.

The agricultural crisis is old news. It doesn't surprise us to hear that 6,500 farmers were expected to go out of business in Minnesota alone by 1999, and that another 40,000 faced losing their farms throughout the Midwest in the year 2000.[8] Disproportionate subsidies to corporate farms and agribusiness, coupled with overproduction and limited trade exports, resulted in financial loss and suffering for many small and family farmers. While this potentially disastrous crisis was largely averted when many of the farmers had crops with high yields that were coupled with last minute federal funds based on these yields, farmers in the upper Midwest remained in a very tenuous situation, to say the least. Many faced increasingly high rates of poverty as well: over one-third of farmers in this area had a household income of $15,000 per year or less,[9] and many felt little hope. Although many farmers seemed stoic, remaining silent about the losses they and their communities were facing, the 1990s caused many to think of the 1980s farm crisis, fresh in their minds as it brought neighbors' suicides, economic change, and broken lives. One of Prairie Town's residents, a farmer's son, explained:

> [T]he biggest thing the [1980s] farm crisis did was it took away confidence, where a lot of [the younger generation], they don't want to live in [Prairie Town], which, you know, in part, that's our fault by saying, you know, you need to get out of here to gain.

He continued:

> A lot of hard times, and . . . it changed the whole economics because we went from a lot of people working, and now there wasn't . . . now we've got to find jobs elsewhere, you know.[10]

Minnesota Farmer's Union President David Fredrickson encouraged Prairie Town's farmers to speak out about the situation they faced at the beginning of the year 2000:

> While we are bombarded with news stories of stock market gains, record company earnings and increased prosperity for middle-income families, whole communities are suffering economic strife. Farmers face record-low prices for their commodities. Main Street businesses are closing. Church collection plates are light. And few farmers are saying a word. . . . If we continue our silence and are content to let things "just happen," rural communities will become just another chapter of America's history.[11]

More often than not, these stories and statistics lead us to believe that farmers and their communities are defeated by the dire circumstances they face. While this may be true in some instances, there is a growing commitment among many rural people to stay close to their rural roots and values, to carve out a new life on the prairie. As Sturdevant noted:

> Economic change in rural Minnesota means some of the people who live there will leave. But others reject the notion of becoming "displaced workers"—at least in the geographic sense. They are determined to stay put, and to find ways to thrive.[12]

These struggles for survival, for defining and writing a new rural life, entail a new rural literacy that changes the ways that rural life, work, and education are constituted and realized. The most commonly proposed solutions for rural communities have typically been economic in nature, involving the neoliberal encouragement of economic diversification through value added agricultural products, agribusiness and telecommunications industries, and other similar endeavors. However, neoliberal policies, such as Clinton's 1996 welfare reform, have had the adverse impact of worsening conditions for poor and working poor in this country. For example, welfare reform has resulted in the poorest families' incomes decreasing when welfare and food stamp benefits were lost as recipients took low-paying jobs. Given the economic recession in 2001, it is clear that simply offering jobs is not enough, and the conditions for these families will only worsen unless living wage jobs with potential for advancement, healthcare, and affordable housing become a national priority.[13] In the same way, the situations facing rural communities cannot be easily resolved merely by providing jobs, and the stark labor shortage that is common throughout the rural Midwest is a testament to this fact. For rural people, it is unlikely that solely focusing on economic solutions will provide the answers they need[14] because decisions concerning emigration from rural communities to urban and suburban centers is tied to much more than the availability of work. While some hope to remain in rural areas because of connections to families and traditions, others leave because of beliefs that life will be better elsewhere. These beliefs are often connected to images and information conveyed through the media and schools that rural life is somehow less sophisticated and in turn less desirable than life elsewhere.

There are many misperceptions about rural American life, often perpetuated by a false binary between urban/rural living. Rural peoples in particular are often seen as independent and self-sufficient,[15] an image that overlooks the community aspects of rural life. Many believe that most rural people are employed on farms, when in fact only 7 percent of rural employment is farm employment.[16] Meanwhile, television shows (such as *Green Acres* or *The Beverly Hillbillies*) and Hollywood films (such as *Deliverance*, and *Southern Comfort*) convey negative messages about rural life as crude, lacking in even the most basic amenities, and militant. Given the ways in which these myths are entrenched in American culture, it is unlikely that they will be dispelled any time soon, at least not without a radical reframing of what it means to live and work in rural communities.

Prairie Town's residents, like some other rural groups across the United States, began two efforts to redefine their existence, indeed to create a new cultural model, during the two years we lived in this community. Prairie Town's people acknowledged at least implicitly the conflicting ideologies and (mis)understandings that exist about rural life and, likewise, the extent to which market forces have spread into nearly every aspect of American life. Some in Prairie Town recognized that change was needed—outmigration of young people, lack of living wage jobs, and uncertainty in agriculture made life tenuous at best for many. Because of these issues and a hope to improve their rural life, the townspeople organized attempts to create a public space where they could work to control this change in ways that would better suit their own hopes and values.

The first such effort toward this end involved strategic planning for the school district. It has been argued that the critical work of change can, and should, begin in rural schools.[17] Schools have commonly been considered centerpieces of rural Midwestern communities, and Prairie Town was no exception to this claim. Education in rural Minnesota has undergone much change over the past century as consolidation, standardization, declining populations, and other challenges have taken their toll, leaving many communities without schools. In spite of this, there are some towns that have resolved to keep schools in their communities, and some are painstakingly working to reshape education to successfully meet the social, political, and economic challenges they are facing.[18] Prairie Town shared this resolve.

In order to address community change both in and outside of the school, Prairie Town held a series of town meetings in addition to the school planning sessions. Sponsored in part by the Blandin Foundation,[19] this effort was grounded in recognizing that Prairie Town's greatest resource is people and that leadership, diversity, improvement, and cooperation need to be addressed in order for community improvement to occur. These attempts, eventually named the Prairie Renaissance, are ongoing and provide hope as the community seeks to redefine its position in relation to the continuing agricultural and rural condition.[20] There is broad consensus across those participating in these efforts that rural life is worthwhile; in other words, there is cultural capital[21] that is of value in Prairie Town.

Over time, the pile of corn near the railroad tracks extended to additional piles on the fairgrounds and in other parts of the town. As my husband and I commented about these piles to our new neighbors, we learned that in some respects, the corn represented a newly emerging rural literacy—one that contained some elements of the past, but more importantly, embodied a hope for the future. This new agrarian literacy is complex, involving sometimes conflicting values for participatory democracy (even though diversity is always not fully embraced), capitalism (including an understanding of market principles of supply and demand, coupled with efforts to control the market in particular ways), and preserving an agricultural and rural way of life that is connected to its past and to others. At the very least, this newly emerging rural literacy is grounded in a resistance to neoliberalism, hopes for economic change, and desires the freedom to choose to live and work in rural communities.

Prairie Town is not alone in its struggle for survival. Other rural communities throughout the United States face similar circumstances. In an award-winning article for *The Nation*, journalist William Greider noted the long-term impact of free-market capitalism on America's farmers.[22] Giant corporations' cumulative control of food production, including the consolidation of crop, livestock, seed, and fertilizer businesses, has increasingly constrained the agricultural market, which is now managed by an elite, economically powerful few. It almost goes without saying that this centralizing trend has taken an especially difficult toll on the small family farmer, whose work is no longer deemed efficient enough by market standards to merit support, whether financial or otherwise. This toll has been exacerbated by the Clinton Administration's Freedom to Farm Act, which attempted to move farmers to total reliance on the market with little to no safety net.

As government policies attempt to move agriculture to a free-market enterprise, all Americans are affected, not just the dwindling number of small-scale farmers. According to Greider's report, everyone pays for the fast food created by agribusiness—costs of production are distributed to communities, and rural regions, with increasingly devastated and hazardous landscapes, become isolated or sparsely inhabited by residents who are stricken with poor health and poverty. Threats to the security of the food supply, including the increasing likelihood of salmonella and other food-borne diseases, as well as concerns about a crisis in supply given the increasing homogeneity of products, are imminent according to some sources.

As Greider observed, most Americans are all too familiar with the common image of a despairing farmer and his wife sitting at a kitchen table, pouring over bills as children cry in the background. One farmer's son in Prairie Town questioned whether rural communities would survive this "conflict" (i.e., the ongoing agricultural condition). Meanwhile, farmers worldwide questioned the future of farming:

> You won't find any more guys like us who went through years and years of working more and more to earn less and less. That's what's been happening for

the past ten years. . . . Now the younger generation doesn't want anything to do with that.[23]

We often think of these areas as defeated, indicating at some level that the traditional farm life is no longer sustainable, while television news segments too frequently carry scenes of farm auctions, with nervous neighbors trying not to benefit too much from their colleagues' defeat as they wonder how long they'll survive. Either nostalgia for Thomas Jefferson's yeoman farmer or disdain for what might be perceived as a resistance to "progress" become the typical emotional appeals to the American public through media depictions of the dire circumstances facing rural communities.

Agribusiness, while rarely explicit in the media, is the ever-growing "free market"[24] representation of rural America. Corporate takeovers and mergers of smaller farms and businesses have become commonplace in rural communities as industries such as Con-Agra, Tyson, Hormel, Iowa Beef Processors (IBP), and others step up their presence in rural areas in the name of the free market, efficiency, and progress. Greider's description of this second scenario demonstrates how the market leaves little of rural America untouched by its presence. Ironically, these corporations ultimately ruin the free markets they endorse as oligopolies become commonplace. Meanwhile, rural schools and children are subjected to the same neoliberal values evident in the market, both in terms of school consolidations modeled after business efficiency and the extent to which schools increasingly prepare students through curriculum driven by the ideology of globalization, which is designed to prepare children for the work in a global economy. Prairie Town's school superintendent expressed this sentiment well when he said:

> Our children need to be able to compete in a global market. . . . We can't just look at what they'll need to live in this community or this region. We need to give them that sharp edge they'll need in the global workforce.[25]

In spite of the growth of agribusiness and the influence of neoliberalism, a third trend is slowly taking hold in rural America, one that is grounded in resistance to neoliberalism and is energized by hope that life can be different. In some areas of the United States, agrarianism,[26] a movement to return to the sensibilities and values that correspond to "land communities," is slowly taking hold. Similarly, grassroots groups resisting agribusiness and market-based principles in rural communities are beginning to mobilize. Greider offered the Organization for Competitive Markets (OCM) as one of several examples of such efforts. This group has organized against pollutants and toxins in the air, water, and soil, addressing the many varied health issues facing rural communities and residents. OCM also has proposed that the establishment of a global food reserve could help to stabilize prices that can vary wildly based on swings of the market. In addition to OCM, Greider noted that the Western Organization of Resource Councils (WORC) unites farmers and environmentalists across six states, while the Pennsylvanians for Responsible Agriculture (PFRA) promotes clean water and air as well as safe food. Interestingly enough, these groups are not about nostalgia for yeoman farmers or a desire to return rural America to the "good old days," but rather embody a hope to establish a new kind of farmer, and ultimately a new rural America. These are but a handful of activist groups who want to move rural communities forward in careful and well-planned endeavors that will provide individuals the freedom to choose to live and work in rural areas.

While nothing is yet so organized in Prairie Town, there is a similar restlessness and potential for change as residents begin to organize and articulate their hopes for the future. Toward this end, some residents conveyed a commitment to rural life, coupled with a hope that their children can similarly enjoy and sustain an existence on the flat prairies of western Minnesota. Prairie Town's mayor, a former elementary school teacher, observed:

> I think that the school is doing a much better job of teaching the kids how to get along in the community, and what's important in the community, and you know, we all have something of value to add. . . . It's good for them to see that at a young age and . . . maybe they'll stick around longer, I don't know. Something we'll have to look at.[27]

Neoliberalism is not inevitable; neither is the demise of rural America. We find hope in Prairie Town as community members question neoliberalism, economic inequality, and the meaning of community. Prairie Town residents recognize, at least at some level, that these issues are social constructions that have ordered their lives, shaping their sense of reality and identity perhaps in ways they don't always choose.

Eventually, Prairie Town's farmers sold the piles of corn when they were satisfied with the price the government offered, and eventually my husband and I, along with our boys, drove away from Prairie Town retracing the nearly one thousand miles back to Pennsylvania. In the time since our return, Prairie Town has continued the hard work of change in its efforts to gain better control over their rural life. The school board passed a strategic plan for the district, hired a new superintendent, and began to plan for a new elementary school building. As I write, the Prairie Renaissance meetings continue as residents redefine their life in this rural community—indeed as they develop a new cultural model. Meanwhile, I've visited a small rural community approximately ninety miles northwest of Penn State University, where I now work, that is similar to Prairie Town in its growing unrest with what they perceive the economy has done to their rural life. This community, nestled along the Susquehanna River in the rural Appalachian mountains, looks very different from Prairie Town on the surface. However, the effects of globalization, the resistance to diversity, the displacement of rural workers to urban areas, and the deterioration of rural life cause these seemingly diverse communities to share much in common. As this small Pennsylvania community begins a series of town meetings and efforts toward redefining its own rural life, much like Prairie Town is doing with its Prairie

Renaissance, they may find hope in Prairie Town's story and solidarity with the rural communities Greider describes.

For many of us, it is difficult to imagine how our lives could be different. Prairie Town's story reminds us, however, that not everything can be bought and sold, and that piles of corn can accumulate if we so choose. Perhaps more importantly this story reminds us that resistance to neoliberalism and globalization and an articulation of alternatives to existing societal structures and dominant Discourses are possible through participatory democratic practices. New cultural models can be constructed that employ new literacies that enable individuals in Prairie Town and elsewhere to actively work to construct ways of being that are consistent with the values of how we all might hope to live together. Arundhati Roy, in writing of the devastating human consequences neoliberalism has had for farmers in India, stated:

> What we need to search for and find, what we need to hone and perfect into a magnificent, shining thing is a new kind of politics. Not the politics of governance, but the politics of resistance. The politics of opposition. The politics of slowing things down. The politics of joining hands across the world and preventing certain destruction. In the present circumstances, I'd say that the only thing worth globalizing is dissent. It's India's best export.[20]

Sharing Prairie Town's experiences, along with the commonalities it has with other rural communities, is an attempt, albeit a modest one, to take Roy's comments seriously—to resist, to slow things down, and to join hands with others. Literacy, multiple and situated as it is, is key to this process. As we begin to consider the possibilities for social and democratic change that is under way in Prairie Town and other communities, an explanation of literacy as it is used throughout this text is in order.

Literacy: A Sociocultural Perspective

When we arrived in Prairie Town, I'd been working for a year on a dissertation tracing how President Clinton's neoliberal policy, America Reads, had been realized in one community.[29] Although I had looked at the ways in which reading was situated in the sites where America Reads was practiced, I was caught in the political rhetoric that reduced literacy to reading and further reduced reading to language sounds and their print correlates. In other words, the "reading wars" and so-called "literacy crisis"[30] brought about increased pressure for school systems to move "back to the basics" (i.e., systematic instruction in reading). Federal and state officials were bearing down on schools in increasingly intrusive ways as legislation (such as the Reading Excellence Act[31]) dictated as never before what type of reading instruction would be acceptable, and similarly which standards and assessment would be rewarded. As I began my new position, I was in certain ways resigned to the fact that standards and high stakes

testing were to predominate in the minds of the university students I would
teach, and subsequently in those schools and families they would later teach.

Yet, as I came to understand, literacy is much more than grapho-phonic relationships and printed texts. Rather, as linguist James Gee[32] has explained, literacy is the mastery of the language of a secondary Discourse. To Gee, Discourses are identity kits that attune individuals' actions and language within
particular contexts. Everyone has a primary Discourse—that of their family.
Secondary Discourses are acquired as we move beyond our family and become
members of different groups, like churches, schools, clubs, and communities. As
we master these various Discourses, we become literate as we learn to read the
world according to different Discourse groups. Because of this, literacy is a
complex social practice in which language, including signs, symbols, gestures,
texts, and actions, is used to mediate and produce culture. The corn piled by
Prairie Town's railroad tracks is an example of one rural literacy. As it accumu-
lated, the corn represented a particular Discourse of farming that resisted government prices and recognized the power that could be realized in a collective
solidarity across a group of farmers. This literacy allowed the farmers to mediate
their role in food production in a way that did not tacitly endorse government
prices or policy, but instead constructed an identity that took a collective position against the government's agenda. Such collective efforts have a history in
Prairie Town and surrounding areas.[33] In the past, the Farmer's Alliance and
unions similarly protested threats to agricultural sustenance, producing a culture
that constructed alternatives and gave voice to those choices.[34] These acts of
resistance met with varying degrees of success, but they nevertheless were mo-
ments of self-creation and mediation. The corn pile, while it draws on these past
Discourses of resistance, represents a new literacy in the sense that this self-
creation occurs within a context that is increasingly corporatized, and it corre-
sponds well with the new agrarian movements and grassroots efforts William
Greider describes.

Because Discourses do not have discrete boundaries, but are instead generative as new Discourses are created and old Discourses are changed, literacy is
likewise always transforming as individuals read and negotiate their new and
changing Discourses within the broader contexts of society. In this sense, Prairie
Town's railroad symbolizes some of these evolving and competing Discourses.
In the early days, Prairie Town's train brought people, resources, and services,
signifying the vitality and progressive nature of life on the prairie. Of course,
some of the original settlers weren't always happy with the people who arrived
on the train, especially those who hoped the community could remain culturally
homogenous. In time, particularly by the end of World War II, the train could be
read as representative of a new Discourse for Prairie Town. Rather than signifying the progress of the rural community, the train instead symbolized the progress of society outside Prairie Town. As the railroad took young people and
products elsewhere—to fight in wars, to obtain an education, to earn a living, to
see the world—it suggested that other places should have precedence over the
small town. In time, the train no longer transported people, only goods, signaling
a shift toward market priorities that valued larger and more efficient industrial

centers, new modes of transportation and shipping, and different immigration patterns as relocation into the community slowed and emigration from the region increased. What remains to be seen is what the train will symbolize as Prairie Town develops a new literacy and a new understanding of what it means to be rural.

Our literacies, the ways in which we read the world, reflect the various, sometimes overlapping, sometimes competing Discourses to which we belong, and these Discourses are largely indicative of our ideologies,[35] our beliefs about what an ideal world would be. All of us have multiple and sometimes antagonistic Discourses, and all of us are literate in multiple ways. Because of this, literacy is more than an individual, psychological act, but is instead connected to social and cultural conditions. Our literacies, which are shaped by the Discourses to which we belong, reflect more broadly on the ideologies we hold to be true. At any given time there are multiple literacies circulating in and around each of us, competing for dominance as we struggle to make sense of the world in which we live. Mikhail Bahktin,[36] in his discussion of language, similarly suggested that utterances represent multiple, competing discourses. This heteroglossia, as he referred to it, indicates that Discourses are sometimes tension-filled as contradictions between the past and present intersect and potentially work to create new possibilities. In Prairie Town, these tensions and contradictions become evident as some community members draw on literacies of the past and present, whether consciously or not, to imagine what may be best for the future. Ultimately these literacies, these ways of reading the world and their corresponding Discourses, represent what Gee describes as cultural models, or everyday theories about the world. He explained:

> Cultural models tell people what is typical or normal from the perspective of a particular Discourse (or a related or aligned set of them). . . . Cultural models come out of and, in turn, inform the social practices in which people in a Discourse engage. Cultural models are stored in people's minds (by no means always consciously), though they are supplemented and instantiated in the objects, texts, and practices that are part and parcel of the Discourse.[37]

These cultural models, or ideologies, in turn, work either to limit or facilitate the ways in which residents of Prairie Town imagine the possibilities for sustaining a particular way of life on the prairie. As such, Prairie Town's rural literacies enable residents to define what it means to be rural, to refocus political agendas, and to set their own parameters for dialogue, debate, and consensus.

To summarize, literacy in the sense of reading the world is not a metaphor. Instead, it is an activity that extends beyond decoding words printed on a page, and it always involves a "multiplicity and integration of significant modes of meaning-making, where the textual is also related to the visual, the audio, the spatial, the behavioural, and so on."[38] As such, this reading involves texts that have dispersed "into objects to be read and enacted instantaneously."[39] In other words, objects in our society can be both things and texts. The water tower that is invariably part of rural prairie communities is no doubt an object, but it is also a text to be read. For some, it may be a symbol of the past (they're often rusty, they have names of the town's founders on them), while for others it may signify pride in the community (they stand tall and serve as a monument of sorts). For others, the towers may signal hope (particularly for those of us who tend to get lost when we're driving—what a welcome sight the water tower is!) as they remain standing in communities that have withstood much hardship. How we interpret such texts depends on the meanings we attach to the signs and symbols that surround us.[40] These meanings are influenced by our ideologies, the beliefs and experiences that we bring to any reading, which in turn are shaped by the various Discourse groups to which we belong.

Meanings are often struggled over, particularly as some groups attempt to gain control over meaning, in turn making their own ideology seem natural and self-evident. For example, across the twentieth century, capitalist ideologies and the corresponding emphasis on efficiency, production, and capacity-building influenced the way some farmers came to understand the meaning of their work—not only how they produced food, but what they would produce. One of the consequences of this struggle has been that some foods and grains have nearly become extinct while "fast food" has taken over the farming industry.[41] For many, foods that may take longer to grow or may take more land or time to tend are read by some as rustic, inefficient symbols of the past that are not worth the time or space they require. In this way, capitalism has influenced and shaped the meaning of farming, while other ideologies, including those who value "slow food" and organic farming, read possibilities in different foods and growing methods, many of which have been marginalized by the more dominant capitalist ideologies. One consequence has been an increasingly homogenized food market, one that is grown in fields with chemicals that are harmful to humans, wildlife, the water supply, and the land.

Today's rural literacies often fall short of effecting any real change in rural communities because they typically overrely on little more than a wistful nostalgia for the past, a hope to return life to a myth of the way some believe it once was. In order to bring change, rural literacies need to be coupled with a critical engagement of the signs, symbols, and texts of our society. In other words, elements of our histories and present need to be read with an eye turned toward the contradictions, tensions, and struggles of the past as the reader works toward considering possibilities for a new future. Without it, the reading of rural life becomes benign, an exercise in futility, particularly to the extent that we can never return things to the way they once were. Further, we must always keep in mind that remembering how things were is a selective exercise—we remember what we choose to remember—and the hope to return life to the way it once was does little more than perpetuate a false hope to reinstate a selective past. Instead, along with remembering, these stories need to be interrogated as these remembrances can help to preserve stories that teach of the past, cause us to reconsider the present, and offer new possibilities for the future. As educator Roger Simon and his colleagues explained, remembrance should be a "practice of learning, a practice aimed at reopening the certitude of our frames of reference for understanding (separately and relationally) the traces of the past and our contemporary relationships."[42] They continued:

A hopeful present requires a continual re-opening of the past, for only such an opening persists as a teaching. Re-opening the past enables a re-opening of the present as something yet to be completed. To take up one's responsibility to "learn hope" requires practices of remembrance, of reading, seeing and listening, of facing testament, that open onto a past that exceeds its idea in the present (in me). This is a crucial pedagogical point. It is only within such practices that the past can *still* teach, can persistently and insistently teach.[43]

If we are to take Simon's suggestions seriously, we should read rural communities to understand how these rewritings of the past have written the present. Reading the world with an eye toward earlier times provides a way to open up the present, ultimately allowing us to imagine a new future. However, at the same time, we must continually recognize that our remembering focuses only on some stories and someone's account of those stories. Interpretations of these stories, including the stories that are part of this chapter and other like accounts, only tell some of what the past was for some people. These interrogations, which necessarily include an examination of the contradictions in order to consider possibilities for new ways of living together, have much potential to become incorporated into a new and critical rural literacy, a new way of reading rural life that values the best from the past, but likewise works toward a new future.

The stories that follow write Prairie Town in a way that reflects values still remaining in this and other rural communities in contemporary times. Some in rural Minnesota still hold to the core tenets of traditional rural life, one that values community groups working in collective ways, education that enhances life in the community, and change that includes the opportunity to resist. Rural sociologists Elder and Conger observed:

When parents and children talk about the virtues of living on a [Midwestern] farm, they invariably mention basic values of this lifestyle—those of hard work or industry, self-reliance and a sense of responsibility, a commitment to family life, social trust and a value system that is not devoted to money and consumerism.[44]

For some, the potential for change in rural communities draws on the spirit of those who engaged in early struggles to establish the community. For others, the potential for change is limited because of a hope to keep rural communities homogenous and exclusive. In spite of these complexities, literacy that helps one to live and work in rural communities is less dominant today, and traditional rural Discourses have been altered as influences from outside rural communities impact the way rural residents read their life. As rural people work to survive and negotiate their culture within the context of a dominant larger society that increasingly attempts to shift the control of meaning out of the hands of rural people, they have sometimes adapted their literacies to reflect the values of broader society, sometimes in ways that eventually contributed to their own demise. Farm policy, agribusiness, and education policy increasingly aligned with the neoliberal "free market" and work have meant that economic conditions have changed and the purposes of rural communities and education have been directed away from supporting the sense of place that was once so valued. Yet in spite of these powerful influences, and in spite of the ways in which some rural residents have made the terrain fertile for seeds that would eventually destroy them, there are those who have resisted. The pressure to assimilate into the values of neoliberalism has not been inevitable for all rural people.

While today's rural literacies are complex in their values, purposes, and contradictions, in general terms, many in Prairie Town read importance in farm and land, a sense of place and family, and look to community for solidarity, expecting education will help people to live well where they are. These themes of farm and land, community, and education run through the chapters that follow, demonstrating how today's rural literacies are part of a larger struggle over meaning as they exist among heteroglossic pressures to read the world differently based on other, often outside influences. In other words, as individuals read and make sense of the signs, symbols, and texts of their rural community, the meanings they take compete with other literacies, with other ways of reading rural life.[45] As one example, neoliberal literacy (the topic of chapter four) has increasingly worked to change the way rural people read their communities by inserting the market logic of capitalism as a dominant value. As such, some aspects of rural life may be read as inadequate in meeting the ideals of a neoliberal America. This is one of the reasons former President Clinton toured poor rural areas of the country during his "Marketing Tour," his effort to call business attention to the rural communities that could be considered "ready and waiting" for jobs. This attention did not take into account the local literacies of these communities, nor did it consider the social and human consequences that particular types of work may bring to these people who had in many cases already been alienated by a democracy that equated success with material possessions and economic wealth.[46] The influence of society outside small rural towns has attempted to change the tone and tenor of life in many rural communities. In spite of this, some have resisted—some by trying to hold on to the past, and others by attempting to define a new future. By way of introduction, we'll briefly consider three rural literacies—a more traditional rural literacy, a neoliberal literacy, and a newly emerging rural literacy that employs a new agency for change—as they surface in rural Prairie Town and perhaps other similar rural communities. Each of these three literacies is discussed in more detail in subsequent chapters of this book.

Reading Rural Literacies

William Greider's discussion of the farm crisis offers insight into at least three rural literacies that are commonplace in Prairie Town and many other rural communities, and any one or all three may be employed to varying degrees as individuals and groups work to make sense of their world. The first, a more traditional literacy, reads rural life through nostalgia for the past and efforts to return rural communities to the way they once were. "Don't mess with my small town, I like it the way it is"[47] seemed to be a widely held sentiment for many who resisted change and hoped to preserve the rural community as it was. This literacy increasingly contained a language of despair as it became more difficult, if not impossible, to retain traditions and conditions of the past. Yet if we listen carefully, we can hear this traditional language surface from seemingly divergent positions. For some, value is found in raising families in small rural communities[48] where everyone knows their neighbors. One of Prairie Town's teachers explained her contentment in being "so small town" and her comfort in knowing that she could "just go out and go into any business and be welcome ... I know everybody in town almost and I feel comfortable."[49] For others, we can find traditional rural literacies in the goals and values of hate groups who seek the isolation and homogeneity of rural locales.[50] As the Aryan nation established its headquarters in Potter County, Pennsylvania in 2002, August Kreis III, the organization's minister of Information and propaganda, explained:

There's no synagogues around here and very few minorities. . . . . It's probably the whitest county in Pennsylvania.[51]

A second rural literacy reads rural life through a language that constitutes mass production, efficiency, and more recently, neoliberal principles. This Discourse values agribusiness, market-based logic, and fast capitalism.[52] These propositions translate into an actual reality in Prairie Town and other rural communities worldwide, as human suffering and hardships result from these values. Inadequate wages and health care are endemic to many low-skill jobs in rural communities. From a neoliberal perspective, rural communities are a vehicle to reduce production costs (i.e., through meat-packing plants located closer to livestock), value-added products are considered desirable commodities, and a labor force is assumed to be ready and waiting (even though there is a labor shortage in many rural communities in the Midwest). This neoliberal logic has infiltrated rural life and education, and has worked to change the complexion and community in rural towns[53] throughout the country.

Meanwhile, a third rural literacy reads rural life with a language that attempts to slow the effects of neoliberalism, to offer more choices, and to develop alternatives aligned with rural sensibilities. Prairie Town's economic advisor explained:

I think it's a complex interrelationship between a lot of factors that are affecting us. I don't think it's a simple solution. I think it's like anything else in life, it's going to take some concentrated effort on not only diversifying the economy, but teaching the kids that there are jobs here, also showing the kids.[54]

His comments suggested that there are difficult issues to be solved in rural communities, but with some hard work, alternatives that would allow young people to stay in the community are possible. For some, these goals are realized in agrarianism and efforts to return to the land in ways that draw from the past, but are not limited to them. For others, there are grassroots movements that work to protect rural people, rural work, and rural lands. Underlying this, there is a recognition that rural peoples are more than consumers of economic goods as these groups attempt to bridge agency and structure in ways they choose.

Overview of Book

Part I of this book, *The Contemporary Rural Condition,* provides a general consideration of rural life in the United States at the onset of the twenty-first century. Economic and cultural issues, particularly the poverty and racism that are endemic to many rural communities, are discussed in the first chapter, while chapter two offers a closer look at farm policies, particularly the Clinton administration's Freedom to Farm Act, as well as rural labor issues.

Part II, *Prairie Town's Literacies,* brings the discussion in part I more specifically to Prairie Town as we consider the literacies that have existed and compete for dominance in this community. From the time of the first European and American settlers until the end of World War II, a traditional rural literacy (chapter three) typified the reading of life in this community. Traditional rural literacy in Prairie Town emphasized a homogenous community, agricultural work, and a sense of place. In the town's early days, as in many midwestern areas, it was commonplace for settlers to remain segregated and isolated from one another. Early communities consisted of members who shared common ethnic origins, like traditions and cultural practices, and similar values as settlers who were most frequently from Norway, Sweden, Germany, Ireland, and sometimes from eastern U.S. states such as New York established exclusive communities. Yet there were many ways in which these individuals collectively worked together. Socialist and agrarian ideologies often worked against the dominance of capitalist influences. For this reason, chapter three also includes a brief historical discussion that highlights some of the early collective groups in the region.

Economic and societal change around the time of World War II precipitated changes in Prairie Town's literacies, resulting in a new cultural model that emphasized neoliberalism throughout the region, a trend discussed extensively in chapter four. Briefly, neoliberalism emphasizes capitalistic economic principles, placing profit-making and market-based solutions as solutions for social needs and conditions. Those who employ a neoliberal literacy when reading the conditions of their world look for signs and symbols of rural life that emphasize key neoliberal values, particularly in the form of goals that pertain to building the economy. In spite of its hegemonic influence, neoliberalism was being challenged in Prairie Town during the time of this study. Some town residents and officials, faced with the possibility of losing their rural way of life, realized that efforts to validate other types of education, indeed other types of literacy, were necessary. The director of the county's economic advisory council spoke at a public meeting encouraging parents and teachers to reconsider the tendency to measure college attendance after high school as a sign of success for the school district and community. Instead, he proposed that there were many worthwhile and well-paying jobs in the county, that the exportation of the best and brightest students to the cities or to other regions of the country wasn't necessary. This public meeting revealed some of the tensions that were surfacing as educators worked to keep the school in the town by promoting school literacy, which would ultimately result in a continued declining population for the region. These tensions occurred within a broader educational context that promoted increased state-endorsed standardization for the school, in spite of nonstandardized resources. More often than not, these centralized standards reflect a belief that there is one best system for public education. In spite of these pervasive influences, some hoped to find ways to keep young people in the area, a notion that did not receive much popular support in Prairie Town.

Part III, *Toward a New Rural Literacy,* considers Prairie Town's future in relation to the literacies that are well established and a new agrarian literacy that is developing in the community. After a brief review of the literacies discussed in earlier chapters, chapter 5 provides a detailed consideration of change efforts in the community as they relate to these literacies and alternative literacies. In particular, there is a discussion of the public forums in Prairie Town, particularly the Prairie Renaissance project, which attempted to draw on the past to link the community to itself and to a new and reinvigorated future that is in the control of the local rural community. The chapter ends with a discussion of pedagogy as it relates to these public participatory practices.

The final chapter considers how Prairie Town's efforts link to communities throughout the country and the world that share similar issues and concerns. The chapter connects the literacies in Prairie Town with those in other rural communities through the development of a globalized public pedagogy that emphasizes shared literacies, shared resistance and transformation, and shared agency.

Part I

The Contemporary Rural Condition

Chapter 1
Rural Community in a Global Village: The View from Prairie Town

Democracy at its inceptions, ancient and American, has always been the out-
growth of an agrarian society; but its old bones now have new and different
flesh. Consensual government can continue in the vastly transformed conditions of great wealth, urbanism, and rapidly changing technology never fore-
seen by its originators; but whether democracy can still instill virtue among
citizens will be answered by the age that is upon us, which for the first time in
the history of civilization will at last see a democracy without farmers.[1]

During the 1990s in the United States, the Clinton administration moved neoliberalism into the mainstream as a dominant political ideology. Clinton's neoliberalism stressed free-market economics as a necessary precondition for achiev-
ing progressive social aims and protecting individual freedom,[2] in spite of the
fact that free markets are highly regulated by the government and are not necessarily free. President George W. Bush's tariffs on 30 percent of imported steel is
just one example of the way the so-called free market has been manipulated to
serve the interests of "America's unprecedented global hegemony."[3] With neoliberalism, economic investment has increasingly assumed priority over social
investments resulting in an increase in hypercommercialism and a whittling
away of the social safety nets for the poor and disadvantaged. This ideology

became a driving influence behind federal policies, reflecting a political shift toward emphasizing market principles that crossed party lines in many arenas, including education,[4] welfare reform,[5] policies directed toward youth,[6] and health care.[7] While neoliberalism's proponents argued that free market capitalism would "raise all boats," critics pointed out that neoliberalism's broad reach led instead to a dismantling of social safety nets, ultimately failing to help the poor and working poor in the United States and throughout the world. Henry Giroux explained the particularly devastating effects this trend had for American children:

> [neoliberalism] is evident in the passage of retrograde social policies that promote deindustrialization, downsizing, and free market reforms, which in the case of recent welfare reform legislation will prohibit over 3.5 million children from receiving any type of government assistance, adding more children to the ranks of over 14.7 million children already living in poverty in the United States.[8]

In spite of the commonly held tenet that the 1990s ushered in much material wealth both globally and in the United States, a large segment of the population did not prosper. Neoliberal policies and the accompanying popular belief that the market would solve the social and economic ills of our times succeeded in forging an ever-widening gap between the rich and the poor, creating a two-tiered system that polarized the very rich from the very poor. One result of this trend was evident internationally as fifty-one of the one hundred largest economies worldwide were not countries, as one might expect, but instead were corporations.[9]

Within the United States, the richest 1 percent of the country controlled 95 percent of the wealth, a sobering statistic that well reflects the crisis facing the poor and working poor in America. By April 1998, the richest American man had wealth equal to that of 40 percent of the poorest Americans.[10] While this vast inequality might have been blatantly obvious in the concentrated poverty of urban America, it similarly could be well hidden in remote rural towns that existed far from the public eye. Whatever the place, a significant number of people from many backgrounds increasingly lived in poverty and suffered its consequences during an era that was unashamedly touted as one of the most economically prosperous in modern history. As the poorest were promised access to work and living wages if they subscribed to neoliberal values,[11] downsizing (i.e., reductions in the labor force) and deregulation (i.e., privatization) turned public, social concerns into individual, private matters. As sociologist Zygmunt Bauman[12] has noted, privatization works to fragment any sense of the collective, resulting in an emphasis on individualism that ultimately works to colonize public spaces and rob all facets of life, including schooling, of shared social responsibility. The results of this trend influence all aspects of contemporary life, leaving little room for "norms to be debated, for values to be confronted, to clash and to be negotiated."[13]

Throughout the world and in the United States, globalization also brought unequal access to particular knowledges and technology as economically poor countries and people were excluded from global discussions and decisions about the economy and social issues. An unashamed failure to adequately address human rights and labor issues seemed commonplace among the power elite, and environmental concerns fell by the wayside. This coupling of economic poverty and environmental destruction came to characterize many rural communities throughout the United States, resulting in widespread ghetto-like conditions in countless rural towns. This chapter, which focuses on rural poverty and racism, and the next, which focuses on agricultural policy and labor issues, offer an explanation of the conditions within which Prairie Town was situated at the beginning of the twenty-first century. To begin, we'll consider the complexities of rural decline that have led to the formation of rural ghettos.

The Rural American Ghetto

Americans' views of rural America typically materialize as idyllic images of rustic landscapes that contain rolling hills, open spaces, trees, and dirt roads.[14] These deeply ingrained myths of rural life mask more than a century of rural struggles that repeatedly have been lost in many communities. Rather than realizing economic independence and prosperity, rural residents too often find their Main Streets boarded up and corporate interests consuming their family farms, while federal policies increasingly work to serve the interests of large communities, large schools, large-scale farms, and agribusiness. Osha Gray Davidson[15] made no apologies for describing countless rural, agricultural-based communities as ghettos, as he believed that it was far more helpful than misleading in characterizing many of today's rural communities. He further argued that the ghettoization of rural America is caused by complex social conditions that should not be attributed to the farm crisis alone:

> what is destroying rural communities is no more a farm crisis than the Boston Tea Party was a result of a tax crisis. The troubles in America's Heartland are symptoms of much larger problems in our society. Unless and until we confront these problems, future generations will be condemned to endure lives stained by poverty in ghettos, rural and urban.[16]

Davidson aptly pointed out that poverty in rural America is largely an invisible crisis. In popular American culture, there exists an image of farmers, particularly those of the Midwest, as self-sufficient and hearty, an image that often masks the decline of rural America. This decline, manifest in outmigration from rural areas, poverty, and a lack of basic social services (including hospitals and schools) among other indicators, has created havoc in many rural communities. Its root cause is grounded in policies of exploitation, most recently imposed as corporations are supported by federal policies that endorse the view that bigger is better. The result is a vicious cycle that depletes the tax base from rural communities, where services necessary for counties to survive are no longer available, making it difficult if not impossible to draw more residents and businesses to their communities. Meanwhile, the government subsidizes corporations under the pretense that competition is healthy and should be rewarded, further endorsing an erroneous view that large-scale efficiency will bolster the American economy and eventually benefit all workers. The scenes from America's highways often deceptively imply that rural America is prosperous and thriving. Rich, abundant fields conspicuously conceal the fact that over nine million rural Americans now live in poverty, while as many as fifty-four to sixty million rural Americans (nearly 25 percent of the country's population) are affected by rural decline. Sadly enough, this percentage has remained unchanged since the late 1930s.[17] Unbelievable as it may seem, hunger and malnutrition are serious issues in segments of this country where people take pride in feeding the world.

As with many neoliberal economic policies, U.S. government assistance to farmers disproportionately supported the prosperous while neglecting smaller, struggling farmers. The result, like similar trends in the general economy, was for large-scale farms to become larger, and for small-scale or family farms to go out of business. Meanwhile, welfare for the rich typically came in the form of international trade that benefited large-scale agribusiness, crop subsidies, tax policies, and government loan programs. With the Freedom to Farm Act, government subsidies were based on acreage and overall crop production. Consequently, of the $27 billion in federal farm subsidies doled out in the year 2000, nearly two-thirds went to 10 percent of U.S. farm owners, including media giant Ted Turner and NBA basketball star Scottie Pippen,[18] because these subsidies were based on acreage and corresponding production and yields rather than need. These policies, and the corresponding lack of access to resources (including technology), parallel many of the conditions facing the urban poor.[19]

These issues lead to what Davidson characterized as a sinkhole of rural poverty, which results in a continued downward spiral for rural families who become caught in a cycle of intergenerational poverty that is nearly impossible to overcome. This cycle is further complicated by a class-selective migration— the tendency for wealthy families who can afford the costs to move away from rural areas, leaving behind those who are poor. In Minnesota,[20] twenty-five of the state's twenty-nine farm-dependent counties have lost more than 10 percent of their population over the past thirty years, weakening smaller trade centers throughout the state and adversely affecting small and rural schools. Aging populations, the exodus of youth to urban and suburban centers, and uneven population growth in counties with lake and forest amenities characterize the population trends over the past thirty years. Meanwhile, farm income has declined dramatically, forcing farmers to become increasingly dependent on off-farm income.[21] This trend is apparent nationwide as out-migration from rural areas compounds social and economic structures in agricultural-based communities, accelerating rural ghettoization. Goods and services become less needed because of smaller populations, and thus become more costly or not available. Health care and social services become scarce, and many rural hospitals are forced to close their doors. Schools consolidate, leaving many communities without nearby schools for their children, and tax bases erode, resulting in less government assistance in areas that may need it most. As the government, both local and federal, cuts public infrastructure, it simultaneously engages in providing heavy subsidies to rich corporations, which in turn consume small and family farms, resulting in human misery and economic despair.

Rural poverty is a recurring issue in the United States, but relatively little is known about this crisis. Those who are most affected by rural decline do not have the power, including access to the media, or the social capital[22] to bring these issues to the fore. Instead, this crisis, and silence about this crisis, is part of an ideological mechanism that works to keep these issues invisible, largely removed from public debate. However, this trend is not inevitable, and all of us are implicated in this crisis to the extent that we allow rural poverty and decline to be obscured by the rhetoric of efficiency, competition, and the marketplace. Those who are most susceptible to poverty in the cities are similarly most prone to poverty in rural areas, including the elderly, children, minorities, and single mothers. By some accounts, poverty may be considered an even more dire issue in rural communities because of how well it is often hidden. Unemployed rural workers make up a significant share of the rural poor population, which means that a higher percentage of the rural poor hold jobs that do not pay a living wage.[23] The result is that the rural poor often become trapped in poverty and, compared to the urban poor, have more frequently lost hope in finding work that will sustain them.

Additionally, the rural poor often receive little benefits from the federal government. While the rural poor make up 30 percent of the nation's poor, they receive less than 20 percent of the federal government's poverty funds.[24] This phenomenon has been attributed to certain policies, such as the Aid to Families with Dependent Children (AFDC), that have been targeted toward single parent families (the rural poor typically have two parent families). Complicating this, many of the rural poor may appear to be economically stable given the farm equipment and other assets they may own. The result is a rural underclass that faces a host of problems similar to those of the inner city—hunger, homelessness, domestic violence, suicide, lack of health insurance, and child abuse—circumstances that are not completely unlike the conditions facing countries that have been referred to as the Third World. Fending off poverty in light of the overall changes in the national economy makes these rural communities susceptible to business and industry trends, particularly the influence of the meat processing industry. Rather than stabilizing the economy in rural communities, these industries exacerbate racial tensions and poverty as "economic improvement" works to institutionalize racist beliefs and attitudes. In what follows, a brief definition of racism is offered, followed by a discussion of the consequences racism brings in rural communities, particularly as it works to divide and exclude individuals from the community.

Racism and Rural America

Racism in rural America is riddled with challenges.[25] Albert Memmi defines racism[26] as a "generalized and final assigning of values to real or imaginary differences, to the accuser's benefit and at his victim's expense, in order to justify the former's own privileges or aggression.[27]" Memmi proceeds to point out that the term "racism" is not adequate to capture the widespread mechanism that it has become, and suggests that "aggression-justification" may be a more adequate term. Similarly, William Julius Wilson explains racism as an ideology of domination that is not only attributable to individuals, but is also embedded in institutional norms.[28] In what follows, as racism in rural communities is discussed, we will see it manifest in both these levels. On the one hand, there is systemic, institutionalized racism that is rooted in the work conditions and structures of rural communities. At the same time, there are individually held beliefs by community members and leaders that reinforce and exacerbate the racist conditions in some rural communities. These attitudes and beliefs have histories and social forms that begin with what Memmi describes as an interpretation of differences, all of which have worked to the advantage of some groups and individuals over others.

Systemic racism, which makes it difficult for members of minority groups to sustain a living on a farm or in a rural community, has a long history in rural areas of the United States. African American farmers, as one example, have suffered disproportionately throughout the ongoing farm crisis. From as early as the 1850s to as recently as 1964, black landowners have been cheated out of their land or driven from it through intimidation, violence, or murder.[29] Recently, the Associated Press documented 107 land takings in thirteen states resulting in 406 black landowners losing more than 24,000 acres of farmland. It is suspected that there are many more such cases, as thousands of additional reports remain either unverified because of gaps in public records or uninvestigated for any number of reasons.

The trend of black landowners and farmers leaving, or being driven from rural land continues to this day. Davidson noted that, in the year 1964, black farmers outnumbered white farmers in at least fifty-eight counties in the southern United States. By 1996, there were no counties in which this was the case. The farm crisis is not new to African American farmers; according to Davidson, they've experienced a farm crisis since the time they began farming. Racism embedded in "the system," from local bankers and business leaders to the U.S. Department of Agriculture (USDA) and its history of denying loans to black farmers and underfunding programs to black colleges and black 4-H groups. Not only must black farmers deal with the same issues white farmers face—low crop prices, natural disasters, and economic hardship—they also encounter serious additional issues that come with being black.

In addition to macrosystemic discrimination against African American farmers, racism toward many groups, including Hispanics, African Americans, and Jews, is commonplace in many rural communities. Racism runs both ways as journalist Stephen Bloom aptly captured in his account of life in rural Postville, Iowa[30] (pop. 1,465). This small rural community was on the brink of extinction when orthodox Hasidic Jews from Brooklyn, New York, and other areas of the country purchased a local meat processing plant and turned it into one of the most successful kosher meat plants in the world. The slaughterhouse essentially revitalized the rural community as it brought more than 350 jobs and increased business and financial prosperity to the community. What Bloom poignantly captured in his work was the polarization between the Hasidic Jews, who were not particularly fond of the rural Iowans, and the rural Iowans, who were appalled by the ways in which the Jews broke their unwritten laws and changed the rural community. These changes occurred not only through the Jews' presence, but also through the influx of packinghouse workers the Jews employed. While the rural Iowans could tolerate the Jews, who they felt were brash and arrogant, they literally feared the packinghouse workers, who they suspected were dangerous. These workers were often migrant farm and immigrant workers who sometimes clashed as rival groups from Mexico, Kazahkstan, and Russia lived and worked in Postville. Murder and crime rates increased, changing the fabric of life in this once quiet town. Eventually, the rural Iowans manipulated a local referendum that essentially voted the Jews out of town by annexing the business from the city's limits. While the annexation impacted little of the slaughterhouse's daily operations, it sent a clear message about who belongs in this rural community, a message that rings through many rural communities with meat packing plants.[31]

Rural poverty and population decline coupled with corresponding efforts to strategically deal with these problems often result in moves to attract food processing plants and similar low-wage, low-skill jobs to rural communities. Major food processing industries, such as Tyson Foods, Iowa Beef Processors (IBP),[32] and Hormel, stand to save much money in transportation and shipment of their supplies by moving their plants near the farms where the produce and livestock are raised. At the same time, rural towns are lured by the possibility of providing jobs for the members of their communities, many of whom have experienced failure in farming and are desperate to find a well-paying job that will provide a living wage. Unfortunately, these expectations are not fulfilled in a manner rural developers often expect. Instead of hiring many resident, native rural community members, the meat processing industry tends to import workers from other parts of the country or abroad. This trend represents changes in labor policies that exploit these new workers, who are likely to be migrant, immigrant, or minority workers. This importation creates a host of social problems, not the least of which is a heightened racism that becomes institutionalized in the policies of the corporations and in the communities where they live. Minority migrant and immigrant workers are often drawn to rural communities because of the promise of work and the hope that the town will be much like the one they left behind.[33] What they often fail to anticipate is the racism and discrimination by townspeople and local and state officials who hope to drive them from rural communities. One of countless examples can be found in Siler City, North Carolina, where many Hispanics employed by the Townsend poultry plant have lived through protests at local factories that hire Hispanics. These employees have been the subject of rallies where David Duke and Ku Klux Klan members call for the immigrant population to leave the community.[34] Sam van Rensburg, a National Alliance[35] leader, explained to a group protesting the Hispanic immigration to Siler City:

> Your city is being sold out for a quick buck by unscrupulous corporations, who are willing to ruin the town your fathers founded. Folks, there is no such thing as cheap labor. You and I will pay for this labor for the rest of our lives.[36]

He proceeded to refer to the immigrant workers as "mongrels" and the "sewer of immigration," while counterprotestors donned signs that read "Love thy neighbor" and "Mexican Americans are as American as you." This hostile community environment not only terrorizes the immigrant population, it negatively impacts the quality of life for all in the community.

Thirty years ago, meatpacking jobs offered some of the highest paying industrial jobs in the United States. However, Iowa Beef Processors (IBP) began "revolutionizing" the business in the 1960s. The company initiated changes in meat processing that included moving the plants to rural communities and creating disassembly lines that required workers to repeatedly complete one task in the butchering process. As IBP's methods caught on, creating a ripple effect throughout the industry,[37] wages began to spiral downward. As Eric Schlosser reported, IBP opened plants in rural communities, avoiding strong union centers, and recruited immigrant workers, who were less likely to unionize. No longer needing skilled butchers, the company set the precedent for a new labor division that eventually resulted in wages falling by as much as 50 percent. Not only is the industry one of the lowest paying in the nation, it has one of the highest turnover rates. Meanwhile, as the shortage of workers persists, the likelihood of injury increases.

The importation of migrant and minority workers to new food processing plants in rural communities can be attributed to the fact that many of these new processing plants subscribe to a "split labor market theory."[38] In other words, employees for these new plants, who might be recruited from locations such as inner city Chicago, southern California, the Deep South, and Mexico will often undermine organized labor because they are less likely to unionize and they will agree to employment at lower wages and lower status. As one example, Tyson foods has been investigated for conspiring to smuggle illegal immigrants into the United States to work in their poultry plants. The indictment stated that such hiring practices were condoned in order to "meet [the company's] production goals and cut its costs to maximize Tyson profits."[39] The logic of a split labor market theory, which also underlies the logic of the NAFTA,[40] is that these new workers will benefit the entire labor process by redistributing the savings they afford the industry to higher status workers, who are typically white and native to the community. This structuralist manipulation encodes a racist policy that works against the overall welfare of the workers and the community, undermining any sense of solidarity or collective possibilities, reproducing human misery for all involved. Meanwhile, these policies propose that higher status and higher paying jobs will be made available and offered to English speaking and bilingual workers. If this does happen (and it rarely does[41]), opportunities for minority workers to secure higher paying jobs within the company become nearly non-existent. Along with this, there is an assumption that cheaper labor will result in lower costs for products and that these savings will be passed on to consumers. In the meantime, racial antagonism increases as workers from a variety of backgrounds struggle to make ends meet and to make sense of these tenuous and often dangerous situations.

Food processing workers rarely earn a living wage, adding to the numbers of rural working poor. In 2001, Schlosser reported that the average worker earned $9.50 per hour, which is higher than the national minimum wage ($5.15 per hour) but less than adequate as a living wage (typically calculated at $11-$15 per hour).[42] One consequence of low wages and difficult work conditions is that these workers typically migrate among or between food processing plants as cyclical migrants, searching for regions with lower costs of living and often crossing international borders.[43] This creates what Hackenberg and Kukulka[44] described as a "disposable labor force," a "new marginal working class" susceptible to monopolistic corporations that fail to provide for workers' basic needs, in terms of wages, health care, and safe work environments.

The Occupational Safety and Health Administration (OSHA) recognizes the food processing industry as having some of the most hazardous jobs in the United States. Never was this more apparent than on September 3, 1991, as one of the most horrific examples of consequences these hazards could bring occurred when fire, sparked by faulty equipment, swept through the Imperial Food poultry plant in Hamlet, North Carolina, killing twenty-five workers and injuring fifty-six. The plant's 200-person workforce was mostly black and mostly women, poor people who turned to the poultry plant, noted for its subhuman working conditions,[45] because there was no other way for them to make ends meet. To prevent workers from stealing chickens, management illegally padlocked doors or locked them from the outside,[46] factors later ruled as a cause of most of the deaths.[47]

The meat processing industry is noted for its high rate of worker injuries, with some plants having more than an 85 percent injury rate.[48] Streamlining production and increased speeds on butchering lines only add to the injury rates. At the same time, many of the new workers in these plants have either not worked long enough to afford health care, or they can not afford the premiums offered to them by the company.[49] Burns, lacerations, amputations, and other gruesome injuries are commonplace on the slaughterhouse floor. Meanwhile, as high staff turnover makes unionization difficult,[50] the likelihood that companies will offer low wages and dangerous work conditions increases, perpetuating a cycle of poverty, injury, and destitution.

Schlosser reported that some American slaughterhouses have more than 75 percent of the workers with home languages other than English. In part, this reflects the fact that "networks" develop among the workers—current employees recruit friends and family to work in the plant, a practice considered "particularly effective" among immigrant populations by corporations that hope to maintain a steady flow of workers.[51] Immigrant workers typically are placed in the least desirable jobs in the plant, and this segmentation of the workforce, coupled with the networking recruitment practices, colonizes new and immigrant workers,[52] institutionalizing disparities along ethnic and cultural lines.

Limited English proficiency, combined with a transient workforce, particularly in the Plains states, poses unique challenges for the rural and small schools that serve meat processing workers' children. Given already deteriorating infrastructure, teacher recruitment, and resource issues that permeate many rural and small school districts, many schools are largely unprepared to handle an influx of poor and/or minority students both in terms of personnel and resources. In a study for the Center for Rural Policy and Development, Greg Thorson and Nicholas Maxwell[53] surveyed Minnesota administrators and found significant resource disparities between small and large school districts. In particular, Thorson and Maxwell found that small schools more frequently had difficulty with physical conditions in the school (particularly acoustics, ventilation, heating, and plumbing), had limited technological resources (including the phone messaging systems, cable television, online library cataloguing, and science labs), limited library resources, and narrower ranges of curricular and extra-curricular activities. The study also confirmed that rural and small town schools have difficulty attracting and retaining high quality teachers. The researchers attributed the decline in rural and small schools to farming and mining crises throughout Minnesota. These schools, with already declining infrastructure and limited resources, seem ill-equipped to handle the influx of migrant and Limited English Proficient children whose parents work in rural slaughterhouses.

Minnesota's Department of Children, Families, and Learning reported that 56,000 children in Minnesota during the 1999-2000 school year did not speak English at home, a 22 percent increase from the 1997-1998 school year[54] with large concentrations of Spanish speaking children in areas with food processing plants. Although urban schools often have already established programs and full-time staff to help educate children in the English language, rural educators have to build English language programs, relying to a great extent on trial and error, limited budgets, and smaller faculties.[55] Thorson and Maxwell called for the legislature to give priority attention to these conditions; yet it seems that for some children, reallocating resources yesterday wouldn't be soon enough.

Within this broader context of rural poverty, decline, and racial tensions, Prairie Town tried to avoid the struggles its neighboring towns and other communities throughout the nation were facing as a consequence of meat processing plants and other large industries that institutionalized racist policies and polarized community members. Prairie Town's mayor explained:

> [W]e think that using our economic monies to enlarge already existing businesses is more in tune with our beliefs than if we'd have to go and spend a whole lot of money trying to lure somebody else here that we don't know would fit in the community to begin with.[56]

Embedded in the mayor's explanation is a covert racial policy that works to exclude minority and immigrant workers from living and working in Prairie Town because their presence would bring unwanted changes to the town. Prairie Town's economic advisor recounted his own experiences with those in the community who hoped to retain the ethnic and cultural homogeneity of the area:

> I was told directly by three of the county commissioners, "don't attract those kind of people here." They're talking about Mexicans, Hispanics of any kind, because we don't want to be like [Grassland, where a Jennie-O turkey processing plant and Hormel Meats are located].[57]

The leadership in the Prairie Town observed the challenges their neighboring town experienced as the influx of Hispanic and Somalian workers brought social and economic changes to the community and school. Prairie Town's leaders clearly wanted to protect the homogeneity of their own community. The economic advisor continued:

> I'd probably lose my job if I [were] to attract a Jennie-O type business that employed Hispanics for slaughtering pigs or something. I know it would come to that. I know it would come to that.[58]

Prairie Town's mayor, while addressing this same issue, said it was "lucky" for them that Prairie Town didn't have the appropriate sewer system needed to support a meat processing plant when Jennie-O was considering her town. Yet, whether there was a meat packing plant or not, some of Prairie Town's residents recognized the need to address some tough issues about race in the community. In the spring of 2000, a handful of local residents gathered at a small restaurant in an effort to define racism and to begin to work to change the climate for minorities in the community. At the same time, community planning efforts were under way, part of which was directed toward overtly embracing diversity. These efforts are taken up in more detail in chapter 5.

Poverty, Race, and the Potential for Social Change

Poverty and racism have been long-standing issues in rural communities, their existence deeply ingrained in the structures of rural life. Being aware of these issues, developing a consciousness about them, is a first step toward change; however, awareness alone is not enough. As Albert Memmi suggests, there must be a continual pedagogy that works to diminish fear and encourage friendships and solidarity.[59] Such a pedagogy can work to not only disarm racist tendencies but also to overcome economic discrimination that works to keep people living in poverty and ghetto-like conditions. Otherwise, poverty and racism only separate people, diminishing their efforts for collective social change. Similarly, as Henry Giroux explained, a critical, public pedagogy provides an opportunity for individuals to consider complex cultural issues (including class, race, gender, sexual orientation, and ethnicity) as they embrace a "radical democratic politics that stresses difference within unity."[60] A central aspect of this pedagogy is the development of community around social justice and other shared concerns. Giroux wrote:

> Pedagogy is about the intellectual, emotional, and ethical investments we make as part of our attempt to negotiate, accommodate, and transform the world in which we find ourselves.[61]

Giroux likewise noted that the pedagogical is a defining principle of cultural politics. He used Stuart Hall's work to explain:

> [P]ublic pedagogy as a struggle over identifications is crucial to raising broader questions about how notions of difference, civic responsibility, community, and belonging are produced "in specific historical and institutional sites within specific discursive formations and practices, by specific enunciative strategies."[62]

William Julius Wilson suggested that crossing racial lines offered one possibility toward this end. His claim that the urban inner city and the rural small towns of America share many common concerns is not ill-founded. Living wages, safe and adequate employment, health care, education, racism, homelessness, and poverty are endemic issues for both groups. At the same time, Robin D.G. Kelley's admonitions that we must address racism likewise ring true in the rural areas of this country. A commitment to uniting and empowering both urban and rural groups is not misdirected; however, there are many difficult issues that need to be addressed in order for the potential of such groups to be realized. Simply uniting groups around common class-based concerns is insufficient in addressing the complexities that each group will "bring to the table" in dialogues that link their struggles to broader issues of democracy and justice. More specifically, the consciousness of those involved in such dialogues must be shaped as the history of social struggles are taken into account and the definitions and assumptions that various groups share are challenged. Without this careful work, efforts for social change will not move far beyond the "more oppressed than thou competitions" that have characterized many efforts to cross race and class boundaries.[63]

Within this context, it is likewise important to reconsider democratic ideals of consensus. Instead of focusing on an all-encompassing consensus that silences those who do not subscribe to the dominant discourse, it seems necessary and important to embrace differences within a set of broader, unitary goals. As Young noted:

> Unity and understanding for a new people's movement will not come from pretending that group differences do not matter, but rather from understanding precisely how they do matter, and so forging an inclusive picture of our social relations. We need to wake up to the challenge of understanding across difference rather than keep on dreaming about common dreams.[64]

Critical, public pedagogy links teaching and learning to social empowerment. It allows individuals to imagine a different, more just world and to work toward that vision as it becomes situated within broader struggles for democracy. In other words, there must be a commitment to learning about others coupled with a common mission to move forward and actively address and transform shared issues of social justice. The current contexts and issues rural communities face often work counter to such efforts, dividing and privatizing the needs of individuals and groups, thus preventing transformation from occurring.

Many have long equated rural life and living with the basic tenets of American democracy—the belief that a plot of land and a plow for everyone would lead to the realization of American ideals, including democratic participation and justice for all. Yet rural life has not been so idyllic, and social issues, particularly poverty and racism, coupled with agribusiness, corporate farms, and market-based agricultural policies make rural life complicated in ways that our "view from the highway" do not reveal. Prairie Town, like many rural communities, has not been immune from these influences, but at the same time, residents have begun the hard work of attempting to change these conditions in ways that will allow them to live differently together. Before turning to a discussion of their efforts, it is necessary to consider the farm policy and labor issues that shaped rural life in the 1990s.

Chapter 2
Agricultural Policy and Labor Issues in Rural Minnesota

Early in the fall of 1999, some residents of western Minnesota gathered for a daylong meeting in North Mankato, Minnesota, just north of Prairie Town near Fargo, North Dakota, to discuss the situation farmers throughout the region were facing. Since 1935, the number of farmers in Minnesota has steadily declined, making some feel certain the family farm will be an artifact of the past, particularly given globalization and corporate control of agriculture in America. Those who survived the farm crisis of the 1980s faced new challenges in the 1990s as commodity prices crashed, overseas markets shrunk, and foreign producers remained protected by their governments.[1] Within the context of these public issues, the group in North Mankato shared concerns on a more personal level—namely, fear that the pressure to "get big or get out" would spur more suicides and violence among their neighbors like those that accompanied the farm crisis of the 1980s. From 1983 to 1988, 913 male farmers killed themselves in the upper plains states alone,[2] a rate that was nearly double the national average for white men.

Agricultural policy impacts life in rural communities in a variety of ways. During the 1990s, the shift toward free market principles in farming meant that rural areas faced sometimes unpredictable circumstances as crop insurance policies were changed and federal government subsidies were altered. In the 1990s as neoliberalism drove the federal government's approach to agriculture, farmers of all types were left with dwindling safety nets and increasing uncertainty about their future and the ways in which agribusiness and the federal government would influence their livelihood. However, the 1996 Freedom to Farm Act did not necessarily succeed in the manner officials expected, leaving many wondering what the market's role in agriculture should be, and ultimately what ways, if any, capitalist agriculture and family farming might intersect. To consider these questions more fully, a discussion of farm policy and labor issues follows.

Global Marketplace: Relinquishing the Family Farm to the Market

Perhaps the most significant shift in federal farm policy in recent history occurred on April 4, 1996, when President Clinton signed into law the largely Republican-backed[3] Freedom to Farm Act,[4] otherwise known as the Agricultural Market Transition Program. Largely considered a response to then-Speaker of the House Newt Gingrich and his fellow Republicans' concerns over "agriwelfare," the bill articulated the means for transitioning U.S. agriculture to a full market system. As one report of the policy explained:

> the new policy presents a reasonable strategy for weaning farmers from government payments and putting an end to Uncle Sam's attempts to "manage" markets. In exchange for the "declining" part of the deal, farmers will receive predictability. They and their bankers will know how much their payments will be. When the program ends, no one should be able to argue that farmers weren't given every chance to make the most of their market opportunities and learn how to go it alone.[5]

The Freedom to Farm Act's primary intent was for farmers to rely solely on the market, not the government, in deciding what to plant and for income for their crops. The federal government's plan was to phase out and alter its support of farmers across the seven years of the bill. The key difference between this government support and past farm policy was that, with Freedom to Farm, the government provided subsidies based on past production rather than offering price security through subsidies that rose as market prices declined. Past federal farm policy also involved control of certain key crops (like wheat, corn, and cotton),[6] as the federal government paid farmers to limit crop production.[7]

Before Freedom to Farm, the government offered subsidy payments to farmers based on market conditions. As journalists Debbie Howlett and Richard Benedetto explained, the government would calculate the number of acres a farmer could potentially plant as well as the yield that could be expected per acre. Then, based on these estimates, cash payments would be determined by subtracting the market price from a target price set by the government.[8] The result was that farmers were limited in their planting of particular subsidized crops, and may even have fields that would go unplanted if the government anticipated a surplus of that particular crop. This practice of federally driven production control began with President Franklin Delano Roosevelt's New Deal in the 1930s. FDR's agriculture recovery program, formalized in the 1933 Agricultural Adjustment Act, centered on acreage limitation as a means to increase farm incomes through direct payments to participating farmers and rising prices that corresponded to production restrictions.[9] Although this practice was intended to be a temporary effort to change the farm economy and increase farm income, it remained a permanent practice. Subsequent administrations, from the World War II era's agricultural expansion, to Agricultural Secretary Charles Brannan's efforts to modify this policy during the Truman administration, the opening of foreign markets in the 1970s, and the farm crisis of the 1980s, formulated no substantive changes to this practice. By the time of Newt Gingrich's Congress, many felt that production control and federal subsidies to farmers resulted in too much money being paid to farmers. The failure of 60 years of programs to provide stability in agriculture and the growing resentment of corn and soybean farmers to the planting restrictions provided political support by some farm groups. Meanwhile, the 104th Congress expected that changes in policy through the market transition in Freedom to Farm would result in the government saving as much as $13 billion dollars over seven years.[10]

Supporters of Freedom to Farm legislation claimed that it was time for Americans, including politicians looking for farm votes, to move beyond their nostalgia for the family farmer and instead to look to the market for innovative and much needed changes in farming. Drawing comparisons to welfare policy, some supporters suggested that there was no economic sense to "propping up" family farms.[11] These arguments asserted that the nation had more farmers than it needed,[12] although only 3 percent of Americans worked in the fields. This figure stands in stark contrast to 1890 estimates that nearly 65 percent of the population lived and worked in rural areas. Changes in technology, including tractors, electricity, management, and seed, along with other modern amenities, were welcomed by farmers and rural peoples. At the same time, technological advancements changed the face of modern-day farming. Increased efficiency and the ability to farm larger tracts of land in less time contributed to need for less animal labor (and subsequently less crops to feed animals) and less human labor. Between the agricultural depression of the 1890s and the economic depression of the 1930s, technology, social reorganization, and economic change began the decline in farm and rural populations that continues to this day.[13] Between 1920 and 1930, 1.2 million mostly young people left rural communities for urban areas.[14] Rural depopulation continued at varying rates throughout the twentieth century as capital was increasingly substituted for labor and as federal policies and officials advised farmers to "get bigger, get better, or get out."[15]

This ongoing demographic shift over the past hundred years was coupled with increased centralization and consolidation of agriculture. As machines replaced human and animal labor, food production became concentrated in the form of increasingly larger farms. Technology brought advantages and disadvantages to rural communities. Yet, rural peoples, who had a history of adapting to, resisting, and/or creating change in the face of agricultural and economic shifts,[16] were less effective in their responses to larger-scale aggregate efforts to control farming. Farmers never had control over the prices being offered for their crops, nor could they influence in any substantive way the overproduction of particular crops throughout the nation. Meanwhile, as business influences increased, smaller-scale farmers accrued increasing debt as they purchased tractors and equipment in an effort to maintain the same levels of efficiency as larger scale farmers. After World War II, however, the dramatic changes in production, coupled with federal policies that increasingly rewarded and protected corporate and large farming complexes, meant that fewer changes could be shaped by the depopulated and politically less powerful small and mid-sized farmers.[17] By the year 2000, agribusinesses came to supply most of America's food, largely due to the fact that these corporations could achieve economies of scale that were impossible for small family farmers. Agribusinesses, through efficiency and cost effectiveness, can utilize the best of today's technologies to produce higher yields for lower prices. Meanwhile, these increasingly higher yields drive prices even lower as supplies outweigh demands, making it all but impossible for smaller-scale farmers to compete. With the continued and some would argue disproportionate support for agribusiness in current U.S. farm policy, which can not afford to let the largest farms fail, the trend favoring agribusiness is likely to continue.

Agribusiness holds more than economic consequences for rural communities. Historian David Danbom noted several contemporary human and environmental consequences accompanying modern farming, particularly to water and soil contamination, as well as the consequences of crop and animal homogeneity and overdependence on oil. The amount of chemicals and pollutants in the ground and water that threaten human and animal health as well as natural resources is an ever-growing crisis. In Minnesota, 30 percent of the state's farmlands and 50,000 households dump chemicals, sediment, raw sewage, and animal waste into the Minnesota River,[18] making it one of the country's top twenty threatened waterways. The extensive wetland drainage that allowed food production expansion during World War II precipitated increased ecological damage to the river, so much so that today deformed frogs, devastated aquatic life, and reduced wildlife and bird populations in the river basin area can only scratch the surface of the extent of damage done to this waterway. Similarly, soil fertility, quality, and erosion are ever-present concerns,[19] particularly as chemicals and toxins from farms increase the pollutants in the land. Meanwhile, the increasing homogeneity of crops and animals[20] heightens susceptibility to diseases or insects that could potentially devastate entire crops or herds.[21] At the same time, agriculture's extensive dependency on petroleum-based equipment and production creates a tenuous situation for farmers as most oil is imported from overseas markets based primarily in the war-torn Middle East.

Critics of Freedom to Farm, including Clinton's Agriculture Secretary Dan Glickman, proclaimed the legislation a failure.[22] The most frequent criticism of the bill was that most of the government monies, exactly like other farm policies that preceded it, went to the wealthiest and largest farmers who, some would argue, needed the money the least. Perhaps the most poignant examples of the disparities created by the Freedom to Farm Act were in Mississippi where 10 percent of the recipients of the federal government's subsidies received 83 percent of the money.[23] In Mississippi, the average payment to a wealthy farmer over a three-year period was typically $217,000. This reinforced the argument from critics such as Chuck Hassebrook, the director for the Center for Rural Affairs, who argued that the Freedom to Farm Act "worsened Congress's tendency to say the bigger and richer you are, the more money you get."[24]

Some criticized the Clinton Administration for not doing enough to open foreign markets after signing Freedom to Farm.[25] Overseas markets first provided substantial agricultural trade options in the 1970s through two significant moves by President Nixon.[26] Beginning in 1971, Nixon made agricultural products cheaper for foreign consumers, an act that was followed in 1972 by an agreement with the Soviet Union to purchase wheat and feed grains. During the same time, there were changes in policies that opened possibilities for trade with developing countries. However, trade with foreign markets slowed in the early 1980s when high prices deterred agricultural exports and foreign consumers began to produce more of their own foods. By 1980, when the Soviet Union invaded Afghanistan and President Carter declared a wheat and feed grain embargo in response, farmers saw trade with foreign markets suddenly spiral downward. This trade never rebounded significantly, even during the economic prosperity of the 1990s. Meanwhile, by the close of 1999, some, including former Senator Bill Bradley, pointed fingers away from U.S. agriculture policy toward other institutions and organizations as they argued, among other things, that the International Monetary Fund's policies caused economies around the world to recede into depression resulting in collapsing demands for U.S. agricultural exports.[27] The same year, the U.S. Department of Agriculture reported:

> U.S. agricultural exports for January-December 1999 were $48.3 billion, 7 percent and $3.5 billion below 1998's value. Imports for the same period were $38 billion, an increase of $800 million. This brings the U.S. trade surplus down from $14.8 billion in 1998 to $10.3 billion in calendar 1999, the smallest surplus in the past decade.[28]

Exports to foreign markets were particularly important to Minnesota's farmers. In fact, over one-third of the soybean crop and more than one-fifth of the corn crop (the primary crops for Prairie Town's farmers) were shipped to foreign markets.[29] Given abundant production surpluses, including large yields of corn and soybeans, and decreases in overseas exports (particularly given the strong U.S. dollar and the collapse of Asian and Russian economies), prices plummeted in the late 1990s. During this time low commodity prices were partially offset by increases in production, which meant that farmers had more to sell, but at lower rates. In spite of this, by the beginning of the year 2000, net farm income was forecast at $40.4 billion, down $7.6 billion from the preliminary estimates for 1999, a $14.5 billion decrease from 1996 when Freedom to Farm was signed into law.[30]

Of course those who suffered most from these decreases in trade and farm income were smaller-scale farmers. Minnesota's Senator Paul Wellstone (Democratic Farmer Labor Party-DFL) stated that the Freedom to Farm Act was "nothing less than a nightmare for family farmers."[31] Meanwhile, the U.S. Department of Agriculture projected that the large decreases in net farm income in the year 2000 would be partially offset by steadily increasing off-farm income that would contribute to overall household earnings. In other words, many rural people who were once self-employed found themselves dependent on work in rural towns and communities, areas that faced low wage rates and limited options (a point, not unproblematic, that will be discussed in detail in the next section). Although farm families were earning income from sources other than the farm, the projected average farm household income of $59,350 for 2000 was lower than the $61,363 projection for 1999,[32] and there was no certainty that this trend would change in the near future.

In April 2000, the U.S. Congress approved $7.1 billion dollars in farm bailout money, most of which went to "fertilize American agribusiness":

Government payments to American agriculture have tripled since the [Freedom to Farm] act was passed, to a record $22.7 billion in 1999. . . . Despite the huge government subsidies, farm income will fall below $50 billion this year for the first time since 1986, the Agriculture Department said. The law did not change the fact that much of the money goes to huge operations growing basic commodity crops like corn, wheat and soybeans for cattle fodder and chicken feed. The subsidies have fueled huge surpluses, sending prices plummeting, and the new law has not helped that situation either.[33]

Although President Clinton expressed concern that the federal government's new approach to farm policy in the form of the 1996 Freedom to Farm Act did not provide enough safety nets for farmers, particularly when they faced hard times, he signed the bill. At the same time, he charged his administration to use the legislation to ensure the ongoing growth of agriculture and environmental improvements and to continue the creation of new economic opportunities for farmers and others who live in rural areas.[34] However, while Clinton argued for significant reform to the Freedom to Farm Act, he was unwilling to allow aid to farmers "mess up market prices," nor was he willing to go back to "the bad old days of overly-managed farm programs by the federal government."[35] Disagreements about what to do with the bill threatened party consensus as prominent figures like Senator Wellstone and Secretary Glickman pointed out its faults. Meanwhile, Vice President Al Gore, stumping the campaign trail for Iowan votes, claimed that it was time to do away with the Freedom to Farm Act and to reinstate cyclical subsidies for farmers,[36] a sentiment he echoed during the presidential debates.

With or without the Freedom to Farm Act, the world's agricultural communities' continually abundant harvests seemed to indicate that crop prices would remain low and relatively unchanged. At the same time, government assistance to U.S. farmers would need to remain high if officials hoped to offset the potentially sharp decline in farm income and the ever-looming financial hardship for many farmers.[37] The surplus of corn, soybeans, and other crops, particularly given the limited market abroad, would continue to drive prices to lower levels, leaving farmers, particularly small and generally less efficient farmers, with limited financial returns for their efforts.

Just a few weeks before the small group gathered in North Mankato, Minnesota, President Clinton in his weekly radio address commented:

> As America's farmers look ahead to this year's harvest, what should be a time of reward and satisfaction is instead becoming a time of disappointment—and for some, for too many, a time of ruin.[38]

Clinton's statements seemed shallow given the circumstances many of these farmers and their communities faced. As the grim circumstances in agriculture rippled through agriculturally based communities, implement dealerships, restaurants, shops, medical services, schools, and others felt the effect of the declining economy. In the spring of 2000, Prairie Town's newspaper reported that "a mood of uneasiness prevails in the local farm community this spring" because many people, to quote one local banker, were "stretched very thin."[39] While record government subsidies prevented widespread farm losses, many were left to wonder how much longer they could hold on. Similarly, as an increasing number of farmers began to rely on income from sources outside the boundaries of their crops and fields, many began to wonder what jobs and options might be available to them in rural communities—or if they would be displaced to suburban and urban areas. One result of these concerns was that labor and wage issues were foremost in the minds of those who hoped to help rural communities survive as these issues directly impacted the off-farm income potential for those who lived and worked in rural areas. Following is a brief consideration of these factors and their impact on rural Prairie Town.

Working for Survival: Wage and Labor Issues in Rural Minnesota

The most common proposal for improving the living conditions in rural areas has been economic progress through diversification.[40] As discussed in chapter one, this typically has entailed focused efforts to provide job opportunities in rural communities, the most common of which have been in the meat processing industry.[41] Small rural towns have often been lured by large industries, such as Tyson, Hormel, or 3-M, because of the possibility of providing jobs for local residents, many of whom have experienced failure in farming and are desperate to find a well-paying job that will provide a living wage.

While to date Prairie Town had resisted intrusion by a large company (whether meat processing or otherwise), the leaders of the community seemed keenly aware of the fact that smaller communities were often vulnerable when seeking to provide job opportunities for local people. Further, as those who traditionally relied on farm revenues as a sole source of income increasingly turned to outside employment to compensate for the economic conditions they faced, small rural towns had to make important decisions about how to best provide alternative sources of income that would both retain and sustain rural families. Central to these discussions were matters of job quality, living wages, and the availability of workers.

During the summer of 1999, President Clinton embarked on his "Marketing Tour" (some called it a Poverty Tour), a campaign that was directed toward calling attention to the poorer regions of the United States with the hope that industry could be attracted to these areas. Clinton stated:

> But we know as blessed as America has been, not every American has been blessed by this recovery. All you've got to do is drive down the streets here in South Phoenix to see that. So what we are doing is going around the country to say we can do better, that morally, now that we're doing so well, we have an obligation to give every American who is willing to work for it a chance to walk across that bridge into the 21st century with us, so we go forward together, leaving no one behind.[42]

There were several assumptions embedded in Clinton's "tour," some of which reflected commonly held misperceptions about life and work in rural areas. In particular, there seemed to be a widespread belief that rural jobs would solve the economic dilemmas of rural residents who, many believed, weren't working. Implicit in this assumption and in the rhetoric about rural jobs was a message about the relationship between work and an individual's worth. In other words, there were those who believed that working hard would help individuals to pull themselves out of poverty; and yet, these beliefs failed to question the quality and wage issues that prevented some rural residents from sustaining a living.

Bill Clinton, both in his role as governor of Arkansas and later as a two-term president, often called attention to the fact that his administration was able to move people into the workforce, largely through the creation of new jobs. Clinton's claims, however, consistently failed to note an issue that was of primary concern to residents in rural Prairie Town and other communities—job quality. In fact, many of the new jobs created during Clinton's tenure, particularly industry jobs, have been low-paying, hazardous, and undesirable. For example, Stull et al.[43] noted that one out of every sixteen new industrial jobs in the United States was in a poultry plant where injury rates tended to be high and wages were likely to be low.

While, according to some reports, the number of jobs in rural areas seemed to be steadily increasing across the country, the statistics that reflected this growth must be read carefully. Osha Gray Davidson explained:

> Since 1990, rural jobs have grown at a rate double that of the 1980s. Between 1993 and 1994, rural employment expanded by 2.8 percent—the biggest jump in nearly two decades—far outpacing the metro job growth rate. . . . But job growth and the resurrection of some towns haven't translated into widespread rural prosperity.[44]

Davidson attributed the fact that prosperity hasn't followed job growth to several factors. For one, he noted that there were so few new jobs in the 1980s that any increase in rural employment opportunities looked statistically significant. However, these jobs often paid low wages, particularly in comparison to similar positions in urban and suburban areas, and there were poor benefits, if any, that accompanied these jobs. Davidson continued:

> A rural worker today is even less likely to earn a living wage than in 1987. As a result, even with both adult household heads working, often commuting 50 miles or more to their jobs, median rural household income actually fell 3.2 percent between 1989 and 1993.[45]

Davidson also noted that the "traditional multiplier effect" where new jobs create more new jobs did not operate in the industries found in rural areas. In other words, the smaller manufacturing plants that often made their way to small rural communities typically bought their "inputs" from distant sources rather than from local purveyors. With the exception of water and electricity, there were few if any local goods that contributed to these businesses, which meant that little or no additional jobs were developed in the community to generate sustainable growth.

Furthermore, rural jobs often offered little job security. What was once a potential market of available, skilled labor in rural areas is now considered to be "used up" or is bypassed as larger companies move their plants to Mexico or other regions where labor is less expensive.[46] Rural poverty continues to grow as policy makers fail to account for the diverse needs of agricultural communities. In other words, policy makers often do not differentiate among the *variety* of farmers who are affected by farm legislation, nor do they easily acknowledge that rural life involves much more than agriculture. This often results in a disconnection between rural needs and rural policies.

Prairie Town's economic advisor, Mark Hartle, was well aware of the labor and job quality issues facing Prairie Town and its surrounding communities. His comments reflect his recognition of the challenges that rural communities face when it came to sustaining a standard of living in rural areas:

> Job quality is really important. I mean . . . it's all related, you look at juvenile problems, you look at problems at home, you look at health problems, it's all related to the economy, and the economy's related to it. If people had decent jobs, they'd have enough money to be able to afford health insurance. If companies were making enough money they could pay for the health insurance for their employees. And I've got a situation right now, if you're working as [a telephone] operator in Chester (a town 10 miles west of Prairie Town), [you receive] no benefits.[47]

For Hartle, a top priority was to provide equitable wage rates for rural residents, as he hoped to lessen the earnings gap between metro and nonmetro regions of the state. Some of his interest in this matter is admittedly personal, as Hartle hoped to have his own children succeed in sustaining a living in Prairie Town. He commented:

But I think that in order for my kids to be here too, I want my kids to have decent jobs. I want them to make more money than I'm making. I'm making more money than my parents did, and my parents made more money than my grandparents. My kids are not, at this point, going to be able to make more money than me. And I don't like that.[48]

Hartle's comments mirror the fact that the American dream has become elusive for many throughout the country. Working hard, which was the Clinton administration's mantra for securing the American dream and becoming a member of "our America,"[49] seems ineffectual for many of the poor in rural communities. Instead, they are working for less than a living wage in jobs that offer little to no security or benefits.

Hartle's comments move beyond his personal concerns to reflect broader public issues of disparity throughout the state of Minnesota. Most of Minnesota's population is centralized in a seven county metro area, commonly referred to as the Twin Cities. The remainder of the state, including Duluth and Moorhead (near Fargo, ND), is referred to as "out-state" or "greater Minnesota." The consequences of this division of the state into two categorically different areas is that much of the political and economic power is centralized in the seven county metro area, leaving rural communities facing more than just geographic isolation.

This point is not lost on some policy makers. Minnesota's Senator Paul Wellstone (DFL) expressed concern about this issue, and in a speech advocating for rural telecommunications development that would strengthen jobs in rural Minnesota, Wellstone noted that "we are already seeing two Minnesotas."[50] He described the emergence of these two Minnesotas as:

One Minnesota would be rural, with decreasing populations, eroding political power, and dwindling economic opportunities for families who might live on the farm, work in the steel plant, or own businesses on main street.

Wellstone described the likelihood that the other Minnesota would be:

Urban, with more over-crowded schools, ever-increasing freeway congestion, and higher concentrations of poverty.

Neither of these two situations is ideal, and yet they reflect a unique trend that has emerged in the state over the past twenty years. Prairie Town's residents were acutely aware of the consequences of this trend, namely the concentration of power and policy making in the metro area. The effects of this dichotomy were a painful reality when public figures, including Governor Ventura, remain far removed from rural Minnesotans. Some became concerned that the concentration of political power and economy in the urban areas would disadvantage rural communities. Hartle explained:

It used to be that [Minnesota's population was] about 70 percent rural, 30 percent metro. Now I think with this census, we're going to find that the metro's going to have the majority. When the metro gets the majority, it's going to be the metro's agenda. And the metro's agenda doesn't necessarily match up with the rural agenda.[51]

While it may be true that metro and rural agendas may have never matched, Senator Wellstone, citing a study by the Center for Rural Affairs, noted two persistent problems for rural communities: widespread poverty and persistent low earnings. Like Hartle, Wellstone recognized that the outmigration from rural areas was attributable to more than failed family farms. He noted:

> People are leaving rural Minnesota due to a lack of living wage jobs. The State projects that many rural counties will lose population, some of them up to 20 percent over the next twenty-five years. Many people are leaving rural areas not because they want to leave, but because they can't afford to stay.[52]

Wellstone and other policy makers expected there could be hope in the telecommunications industry. Because jobs in telecommunications are not necessarily tied to a particular place (such as an office building in a suburban or urban complex), there seemed to be a general belief that rural workers could easily participate in these opportunities. However, for those who live and work in Prairie Town, the answer is not so straightforward. Contrary to what some may believe about the need for jobs in rural communities, a lack of an available workforce, commonplace in many rural regions in the United States, complicates these matters.

Prairie Town has one of the lowest unemployment rates in the state of Minnesota. Mark Hartle reported that unemployment was consistently less than 2 percent for the past decade and was as low as 1.2 to 1.4 percent at the beginning of 2000. He countered an assumption often held by outsiders, including President Clinton, that there is an unemployed, skilled labor force waiting for jobs to come to rural communities. He explained:

> I mean, we look at the participation rates of females in [Prairie Town]. We do a survey where [we find that] half the work force is female. There's something like 5,700 job positions, half of them are held by females. People are thinking, well I can hire some farmer's wife, [but] they're already working. I mean they [think they] can hire some farmer during the weekend, and at night, and in the winter—[but] they're already working. Everybody's working who wants a job.[53]

Traditionally, women were the first family members to seek off-farm work when financial needs demanded extra income. Women found jobs as teachers, nurses, or housekeepers, sometimes moving far from their homes in order to help support their families and family farms.[54] The fact that women held half of the jobs in Prairie Town would be no surprise to those familiar with rural labor issues.

Hartle was also aware of changes in Prairie Town precipitated in part by NAFTA and globalization. He explained:

Things are changing too. . . . It has to be. You have to act locally but think globally. We're in competition with the world. We're not in competition with Fergus Falls or Alexandria, or Watertown, SD, or Omaha, we're in competition with Seoul. We're in competition with Saudi Arabia. We're in competition with the world. So if you look at this situation, we have to put our eggs in separate baskets. And to rely strictly on agriculture, talk to any of the lenders, and they've seen what's coming. Talk to any of the ag professionals, and they know that the trend is not going to reverse. The trend is continued since the 1890s, and it will continue so that you will eventually see farms with hundreds of thousands of acres instead of fifteen to twenty thousand acres, because economies of scale are the only thing that work.[55]

Meanwhile, in order to counter the effects of the rural condition, residents of Prairie Town have been encouraged to "sell" their way of life in order to sustain it. As Prairie Town's mayor explained:

[T]hat meeting I was at this morning . . . was on tourism and agriculture, and one of the things that was mentioned was that we've got to sell . . . not only what we're doing here, but our way of life. And that should be one of our big components that would make people want to come here, because of our life-style and the values are different than they are in many places . . . and you don't think about that, and it really is. And it's up to us to sell that, I guess, and let people know that.[56]

Prairie Town is not the only area contemplating this type of decision. In fact, Governor Tom Vilsack of Iowa introduced a new strategic plan to boost the state's population by the year 2010. This new plan included retaining current residents, recruiting immigrants, and increasing tourism, among other things.[57] While long-range planning is certainly an important endeavor, there were many questions about these decisions that remained unanswered. Certainly we must wonder what a translation of rural life into a commodity might mean for rural people. Beyond this, we must also consider who is making these decisions and how they might materialize differently if others were involved in articulating an ideal vision for these rural communities.

The folks who gathered in North Mankato seemed to have an omniscient sense of the things to come. While the demise of thousands of family farmers was largely averted in 1999, there was a general sense that the federal government's last minute aid to farmers was a bandaid that would not hold for long. As rural officials and residents struggle with how to best preserve their way of life, whether through living wage campaigns or the commodification of rural communities, many are left only with hope for better times. It is within this broader context that Prairie Town began to work toward change. In order to better understand their efforts, we will begin by considering the rural literacies that co-exist and compete for dominance in this community.

Part II

Rural Literacies

Chapter 3
Traditional Rural Literacy

> I thought of how this prairie country is gobbling up the men who settled it, and tamed it and farmed it and built this community; and as the old ones disappear from this land, so too are their farm places disappearing, and the groves and every sign of habitation disappearing too; and even today, kids don't know about places like "Muehlbauer's," "Martin Shelstad's;" and "Thielke's grove" is only a geographic location which marks a good place to hunt deer.[1]

Traveling the back roads that extend from Prairie Town throughout western Minnesota can be quite an adventure. The prairie rolls seemingly endlessly, beautiful in its vastness and expectancy, and you sometimes fear being lost until you catch the faint glimpse of a tall water tower in the far off distance, a reassuring sign that a town is nearby. Some of these towers are rusty now, serving only a handful of people, but they still proudly boast their towns' names in large block letters for all to see—Herman, Alberta, Donnelly, Hoffman, Graceville.

Part of the adventure of driving the wide flat prairie roads includes wondering about the people who settled there, some whose names remain on the water towers. Many of them lived in unimaginable conditions, sheltered by dugouts or sod houses until they could plant trees and build lean-tos and other structures that would help to sustain their life. The early farmers often settled side-by-side with members of the Lakota, Dakota, and Chippewa nations, sometimes living in fear, sometimes in solidarity, and sometimes in battle. The rolling prairie grass still contains artifacts from those days—broken tools, arrowheads, buffalo horns—and stories abound about the not-so-long ago residents who used them. Old timers still tell of the fortitude of their forebears, how they weathered blizzards and wind to work an untamable land, how women wore out their aprons twisting hay to keep fires going for warmth, how grasshoppers came to devour the crops, and how the low lands and swamps flooded when the winter snows and ice melted in springtime. There are happy stories too—tales of the love and strength and good humor that sustained the settlers through difficult times. These stories are often told with a wistful nostalgia for the old days, and many of their lessons remain in the hearts and minds of the old and young alike as they consider what might become of their rural life in the days ahead.

Prairie Town's early stories, some of which are told in this chapter, reflect a traditional rural literacy in this community, a way of reading rural life that has an eye to the past. Stories and symbols of the past, selective as these historical accounts may be, influence life in Prairie Town to this day, and these are often read against present circumstances in ways that point to what many find to be inadequacies in today's rural life. As such, some hope to return rural life to its earlier "glory," expecting this will solve the ongoing rural condition and its correlates (including poverty, infrastructure needs, and labor issues). This chapter shares some of these symbols and stories,[2] along with the language, lessons, and values embedded within them that influence the traditional rural literacies, a reading of the world that has an eye to the past, in Prairie Town.

The chapter is organized around three themes: farm and land, community, and education. Within each of these three areas, the symbols and texts of the past are considered as we work to understand historically how rural life was read by some of these early groups, which in turn shapes the way many still read rural life today. As we've discussed earlier, literacy as reading the world considers objects as both texts and things.[3] As texts, the objects (including the signs, symbols, and texts of rural life) are read in an effort to make sense of the world. The signs rural residents attend to and the interpretation of those signs involve a struggle over meaning. In earlier days, most of these struggles were ideologically based as rural peoples negotiated and contested meanings of democracy and agrarianism, capitalism, and socialism. These negotiations are discussed in what follows, particularly in relation to the various cooperatives and other community groups that attempted to stabilize and secure rural life in spite of the often unstable characteristics of agricultural-based work and a market-based economy. In addition to these groups, there were others who more overtly contested the language and meanings of rural communities. For this reason, there is a discussion of two groups, the Country Lifers and the Farm Bureau, and their expectations for rural regions of the country. These groups identified "rural problems" and proposed solutions to those problems that were sometimes read differently by rural peoples than these "outside experts" perhaps anticipated. To begin, we'll consider how land and farm symbolized hope and stability in early Prairie Town.

Reading Farm and Land

Each man of the land comes and has his time. He lives, and loves and laughs, and walks the land, and calls it his. After a time, one way or another, the man leaves. The land remains. . . . My grandfather . . . came to this place . . . in 1871. He filed a Homestead Claim of 80 acres. . . . He spent the first winter in his sod house. . . . This Homestead Claim is dated 24 June 1878. It is signed by President of the United States, Rutherford B. Hayes. . . . In 1890, [grandfather] filed a tree claim of 160 acres. . . . All of the original buildings and most of the trees have now been cleared . . . except for the steepest ground, this land is under tillage, and is farmed in the year 1978, by [the same family].[4]

The rich black prairie soil attracted farmers from around the world who read hope and possibility in the potential of land ownership and agriculture in the rural Midwest. The young democracy of this country evoked a language that espoused possibilities in land ownership and the democratic participation that land ownership would bring. Although we'll see in what follows that this hope was never fully realized for all people, the farm and land symbolized a way of life that was read as consonant with democratic ideals of life, liberty, and a pursuit of happiness. These tenets did not necessarily have a shared meaning, and were instead understood differently by different groups. Many of the European farmers who settled throughout rural Minnesota found the socialist and populist ideals they carried with them to be in conflict with the capitalist democracy forwarded by federal and state governments and growing industries in the area. In other words rural Minnesotans' commitments to government ruled by the people, where the people collectively struggled to maintain a shared way of life, often conflicted with other groups' efforts to make a profit and corresponding policies that increasingly placed the wealth of the country in the hands of a dominant few.

Many early settlers in and around Prairie Town had a strong commitment to place, coupled with hope to pass on an inheritance of land ownership to their children. This was true in spite of the fact that by 1880 over one-half of the farmers in Minnesota were foreign-born themselves, having moved from their home lands to the prairie region in search of a better life.[5] One rural ideology that was dominant among farm families during this time encouraged children "to succeed them" rather than "to succeed" by rising in the social system.[6] These families, particularly those of German origin, stressed a "generational continuity," emphasizing farming over monetary gain, along with its perpetuation through successful management and operations that would cross generations of families.[7] At its base, these values manifested themselves as an agrarianism that included more than food production, reflecting an ideology that included a set of loyalties and hopes that would allow farm families to live on the land and take care of their own. Families employed a variety of strategies to pass on their farms to younger generations, the most typical of which involved having a son who was farming the land take over the family operations when he married.[8]

Given the dominant agrarian ideology, farming was more than an occupation; it was a way of life. Family ties, community structures, and the cyclical work bound to nature and the land made farming a lifestyle choice. Early American agrarians, particularly Thomas Jefferson, touted this lifestyle as necessary for the success of a democracy. Jefferson claimed that yeoman farmers would form the cornerstone for American democracy.[9] Likewise rural historian David Danbom[10] observed the superior place farmers had in American culture during the country's early days as they provided for the most basic of human needs. Since they owned property, farmers were considered to be self-sufficient and independent, and they were respected because of their closeness to nature, which some felt brought closeness to God. In spite of these idyllic claims, there were stark disparities between the rich and poor property owners, and as we saw in chapter one, between white and black landowners. Further, the patriarchal and exclusive structures of early American democracy meant that only some could participate in the governance of the country.

By the early 1900s, family farms were a symbol of strength and unity for dominant groups in rural communities.[11] Spring plantings, fall harvests, food preservation, and animal husbandry and care joined all family members, from the youngest children to the oldest adults, as they strove to sustain their existence. Historian Mary Neth explained:

> the labor of all family members was crucial for the economic survival and prosperity of small, family-owned farms. Because the vagaries of weather and markets made farm income highly variable, farm families compensated by designing labor-intensive strategies that met many of the needs of the farm and family, and saved cash. Family members' return for their labor came not through an individual wage, but through a share of the living the farm provided and an assurance that the farm would be a resource for the family's future. Farm people viewed their labor not as an individual effort but as part of a group effort, related to the work of the entire family. On the other hand, the authority structures of agriculture and family gave power to the male head of household, who represented the family in the larger political and economic world. Men controlled resources and economic decisions, and thus families were dependent on men. Except in rare cases, women had access to the most critical resource of farming—land—only through their relations with men. These patriarchal structures made familial relations hierarchical, not mutual, and created the potential for an unequal distribution of labor and rewards within farm families.[12]

Women often found themselves with the responsibility of "making do" during tough economic times, working to meet household needs and feed families with little to no resources. While farm work was often clearly demarcated along gender lines, need often superceded traditional roles as women and men engaged in mutual labor to meet the demands of their work. One Minnesota woman wrote:

On the farm, I have always put my shoulder to the wheel and have helped whenever my help was needed in milking and feeding calves and hogs and always felt I was a woman and fulfilling my mission in life.[13]

A traditional rural literacy reads farm and land as symbols of a lifestyle that had particular hopes (land ownership that crossed generations of a family) and value (this land ownership would bring particular privileges within an agrarian democracy). The role that families played in sustaining an agrarian life were likewise read as integral to the success of farms. Yet, these texts, symbols, and language of the past are more complicated than they may at first appear, and contradictions are evident if we read them closely. For example, in time, valuing farm and land was often compromised by increased attention to mass food production, coupled with corresponding efforts to make farming more efficient and to turn a profit. Leveling and tiling the land to make it flat, draining lakes to provide more land for farming, and the eventual use of chemicals contributed to disasters that ranged from the Dust Bowl to pollutants in the soil, water, and air. While the land was valued, it was not always cared for, and the purposes that were embedded in its value shifted for some from a symbol of independence to a symbol of capitalist endeavors. Similarly, while families seemed to be a priority, and land ownership was expected to cross generations, not every family member was considered equally, nor did all share the same status. Women didn't typically own land, placing them in a different position in relation to men, and many farmers' daughters were displaced from the family farms, some in loveless marriages and others in jobs cleaning homes in towns or teaching school to rural children.

These struggles over the meanings of farming and the agrarian ideology in relation to democracy extended beyond the farms and families to the communities and networks that existed across rural people in the rural Midwest. Similar tensions about the meaning of farming and farm life surfaced in tensions about how rural people should live together. The community became a place where the language of farming was struggled over and contested as socialist and capitalist ideologies were negotiated and sometimes controlled by those who lived in rural areas. With these points in mind, we'll extend our discussion from farms and families to consider the structure and values of rural communities, with particular attention to the groups that tried to organize these communities.

Reading Community

One old Norwegian lady once said that all of her children had married well but one. But then it wasn't so bad. He married a Dane and they were almost like Norwegians.[14]

Like farm and land, communities can be read, particularly the ways in which individuals organize and choose to live together. Some communities are more inclusive than others, some share responsibilities differently, and some have different collective goals. During Prairie Town's early days, for instance, it was commonplace for settlers to remain geographically segregated and isolated from one another. Prairie Town, which began as a tent settlement, quickly divided into groups based on economic class distinctions, religion, ethnicity, culture, and race.[15] In fact, it is reported that few marriages in Prairie Town's early days ever crossed ethnic boundaries, even among those who shared a common European ancestry. Traditionally, rural Midwestern communities were sectarian in nature, subscribing to a political localism that was often defined by religious groups and was typically exclusionary.[16]

Transient as the Midwest may have been, it was ultimately "the propertied minority"[17] who came to define rural communities and their exclusionary aspects. The small groups of property holders' values controlled cooperatives, schools, churches, and the character and direction of their communities.[18] Their policies supported the goals and interests of the wealthy in the community, and in many ways, corporate farms and agribusinesses of today could be considered a natural extension of the ways in which the propertied minority dominated the rural community. In this way, neoliberalism is not really new to rural people, but is instead an exacerbation or a heightened form of the capitalism that existed from the early days of these communities.

Market capitalism was highly decentralized in Prairie Town's early days, as it was in many agrarian communities, and the primary economic entities were individual farmers who hoped to sustain their own and their families' existence and to perhaps turn a profit through the sale of some goods. Even these early farmers seemed aware of the inequities, political, economic, and otherwise, that inevitably accompany market capitalism. In the competition to foster economic gain, some in the community would be prosperous, often at the expense of others. In other words, the propertied minority could afford to hire, and potentially exploit, the farm laborers who migrated into town during the threshing season. At the same time, the propertied minority, to the extent that they were smaller-scale producers, could potentially be exploited by larger industries that might charge higher rates for seeds and equipment, or could purchase their goods from larger farms that could sell at lower prices. In order to limit the potential of such exploitation, both the exploitation of others and the exploitation of themselves by larger industries outside Prairie Town, some made a concerted effort to focus on matters of economic equity and the development of a collective social conscience. Typically these efforts materialized in the variety of grassroots movements that surfaced in the town.

As rural researcher Paul Theobald has noted, the traditional historical interpretation of these early settlers typically emphasizes their isolationist, individualist attitudes. While it may be true that many of the settlers in the Midwest chose to live on geographically isolated farms where they looked for markets that would help them turn a profit, many had a strong commitment to community. [19] Because life on the prairie wasn't guaranteed to result in any measure of success or security, particularly given the unpredictability of the market and weather, many banded together to help stabilize their existence by forming various cooperatives and alliances. These populist groups were an attempt to unite individuals together around common interests. Over time, various groups helped to define and secure communities throughout the early 1900s in rural Minnesota. These groups[20] are important to understand because their influence has helped to shape the way rural people read community and its possibilities, and their stories serve as reminders of the possibilities for collective organizing for those who seek change in Prairie Town in contemporary times. One of the first grassroots attempts to control the way rural communities operated within the larger context of a market-driven economy was the cooperative store, one of a series of groups that worked to shape the content and form of rural communities throughout Minnesota and many other rural regions. It is with this group that we'll begin a brief discussion of grassroots efforts.

Cooperative Stores

One of the earliest movements that influenced rural Minnesota communities was the cooperative store. Between 1870 and 1940, cooperatives played a significant role throughout Minnesota. As voluntary associations, cooperatives used democratic practices to control business and the marketplace. Many cooperatives began at the local country store, linking farmers and the market. According to historian Steven Keillor:

> A rural cooperative was a business in a free-market economy, but it remained a democratic institution with its own internal politics. Though a business, it often shaped farmers' adaptations to new forms of agriculture. Committed to neutrality in partisan politics through its bylaws or customs, it often could not escape the politics of agrarian protest. Membership in any given cooperative was usually open to anyone, but members often belonged to the same ethnic group, and the cooperative preserved ethnicity.[21]

According to Paul Theobald, cooperative groups attempted to make community life a dominant value, primarily because they felt individualism would jeopardize democracy.[22] Elements of socialism were at work through the cooperatives, particularly the implicit ideological belief that people, not markets, created their own circumstances and that collective solidarity would bring power to direct and shape these circumstances. Although cooperatives did not have one universal form, they did help to shape change throughout Minnesota, including "farmers' adaptations to new forms of agriculture."[23]

Cooperatives were deemed more likely to succeed if organized for consensus. In other words, they worked best if there was a focus on a small subset of the population with common characteristics, interests, and traditions.[24] Keillor suggested these traits were possible in immigrant communities throughout Minnesota, but not among "Old Stock" Americans who had "too many competing interests, too many economic options, too much hope in political solutions, and too great a reliance on legal guarantees to succeed for long with Union stores."[25] While the growing accumulation of corporate power coupled with the federal government's facilitation of its use contributed to the demise of many coopera-tives,[26] these groups took on various forms that extended from their origins in country stores, including Grange flour mills and warehouses, and cooperative creameries and elevators. Their original purpose, to insert collective concerns as a primary impetus for social action, eventually influenced the formation of farmers' unions and political parties. In this way, they inserted socialist ideolo-gies into the goings-on of community life in rural regions, encouraging residents to read communities in ways that looked toward the collective for solutions. Before turning to these efforts, we'll briefly consider the Grange's influence on rural Minnesota communities. Although the Grange was not a long-lasting entity in rural Minnesota, it is significant because of its influence on later collective and grassroots organizations.

The Grange

The Grange period in Minnesota, which was relatively short-lived, began in 1868 and peaked between 1872 and 1874. During this time the Grange counted its influence on Cushman Davis's nomination for state governor, the start of the Anti-Monopoly Party, and the election of several farmers to the legislature among its successes.[27] Founded by Oliver H. Kelley, originally from Boston, the Grange, unlike rural cooperatives, appealed to Old Stock Americans with agrar-ian-republican ideals. Republicanism, with its emphasis on collective self-government and pursuit of a common good, endorsed a view of citizenship as active participation in self-rule.[28] The Grange was an attempt to realize these ideals, and through secrecy,[29] ritual, exclusiveness, and the inclusion of women, it attracted a following of farmers and nonfarmers alike that eventually resulted in 538 units in Minnesota.[30] However, as Keillor observed, the Grange's appeal to "Old Stock" rather than new immigrants weakened its support in Minnesota, and factionalism, controversy, and the failure of joint purchasing[31] efforts and political programs[32] eventually led to the group's irreversible decline in the state. In spite of its lack of longevity, it influenced subsequent cooperative ac-tivities it sponsored, including the Farmers' Alliance.

The Farmers' Alliance

In Prairie Town, Carrington Phelps, a lawyer who moved to the county to farm and also work as the president of the First National Bank, established the first Farmers' Alliance in the late 1800s. The alliance, organized around a series of meetings and papers related to cultivation and fertilization, was a direct re-sponse to farmers struggling to make ends meet. The group was the first of many begun because farmers were feeling exploited by the government, the rail-roads, and bankers who they felt had little interest in farming.[33]

The alliance, like the Grange before it, experienced controversy around its economic and political efforts, but it differed from the Grange in its recruitment of immigrant farmers, its use of newspapers, and its avoidance of merchants and political elites.[34] Technology, including railroads and telegraph machines, coupled with increased economic centralization, produced different obstacles and possibilities for the alliance. As suballiances formed, those with self-selected boundaries, particularly along ethnicity and religion, "functioned more smoothly than those that followed political lines."[35] These suballiances often became involved in protesting local issues at the county seat, activities that ultimately affected their collective marketing and joint purchasing abilities. Local merchants sometimes resented the alliance and some of the suballiances because they would make purchases where they could obtain the best prices rather than supporting local retailers.

Keillor identified the Farmers' Alliance's democratic processes as inefficient, particularly because a general lack of expertise and the need for suballiances to approve decisions resulted in an overall failure of the alliance's efforts. By 1890, the Farmers' Alliance merged with the National Farm Union. Before discussing the Farmers' Union, however, we'll consider the Non-Partisan League, which was influenced perhaps more than any other of these early groups by socialist ideologies.

The Non-Partisan League and the Democratic Farm Labor Party

By the early 1900s, a more controversial organization, called the Non-Partisan League, was established in Prairie Town. This group, which began in the Dakotas and spread throughout the region, advocated for state ownership of farm elevators, something members felt would better serve farmers in the region. The Non-Partisan League was considered to be one of the most influential radical farm organizations[36] in the early part of the century; however, during World War I, the group criticized the war efforts, in part because of the industrial capitalism that corresponded with the war efforts, and subsequently lost popular support.[37]

In spite of this, the Non-Partisan League did lay the groundwork for the later formation of the Farmer-Labor Party. This group was critical of capitalism, like the Non-Partisan League, because many felt capitalism served the interests of larger industries and businesses more than it did the local communities and family farmers. Larger granaries and larger farmers were able to offer lower prices because of efficiencies of scale; in other words, the more a larger farmer produced, the lower his prices because costs of production were relatively less. These lower prices could not be offered by smaller-scale farmers, who in turn found either limited or no market for their goods if they expected to make a profit. Similarly, purchasers, who were typically middlemen who bought from the farmers and sold for a profit to larger organizations, sought products for lower prices, further endorsing the efficiencies of the larger scale farms. The Non-Partisan League's proposal that the state should own marketing facilities (including elevators, flour mills, packing houses, and cold storage plants) was an effort to wrest control away from these middlemen and in turn to collectively protect the farmers from exploitation. Driven by a socialist ideology that hoped to place the means of production in the workers' hands rather than in the control of a few capitalists, the Non-Partisan League hoped to make production benefit the common good rather than provide profits for a few individuals.

In spite of their dislike of market-based capitalism, Farmer-Labor Party members found alternatives in cooperatives rather than the socialism that defined the Non-Partisan League's platform. In other words, they were not prepared to embrace a collective struggle that would distribute wealth more equally. The Farmer Labor Party still exists today as the Democratic Farmer Labor party (DFL), and it continues to hold to its early beliefs that family farms must be preserved. Further, they endorse the view that rural communities' economic well-being must be sustained through the preservation of small businesses, family farms, and fair prices for agricultural products.[38]

The Farmers' Union

The Non-Partisan League was followed by the formation of the Farmers' Union in Prairie Town in the early 1940s, reflecting local farmers' increasing dissatisfaction with low commodity prices. To protest these low prices, this group decided they would not ship their produce or livestock until a fair price was secured. This marked a time of violence in Prairie Town as farmers who were members of the union tried to enforce their self-imposed no-shipping edict on those who were non-union. Delivery and stock truck tires were slashed, rocks were thrown at trucks delivering goods and livestock out of Prairie Town, and neighbors turned against one another.

The National Farmers' Union, organized from the grassroots level,[39] worked to improve farmers' income and rural living standards, and many joined because of these goals and an understanding that they "couldn't get somewhere alone."[40] In Minnesota, the union linked various cooperatives into loose federations in order to help protect their members, and they were actively involved in local concerns, including getting electricity to various areas of the state. Yet at the same time, they channeled their efforts into education and larger political and protest activities.

Today, the Minnesota Farmers' Union still has much popular support, with 13,000 farm families as members throughout Minnesota. Active in political aspects of agriculture and rural life, the group continues to advocate for family farms and improved economic conditions. Most recently, Minnesota's Farmers' Union rallied in Washington, D.C. to protest the Freedom to Farm Act, seeking changes to benefit small farms, including price caps on subsidy payments to farmers. It has also attempted to build stronger alliances with banks and unions.

All these groups, from the early cooperative store efforts to today's Farmers' Union, offer histories and public memories to Prairie Town's rural people. At the same time, these groups' stories, and the ideological struggle between capitalist principles and socialist aims, point toward a second aspect of traditional rural literacy—the tendency to read rural communities with the expectation that there would be some collective efforts. The various collective groups that were popular in the early days in rural Minnesota and the actions resulting from their attempts to control markets and subsequently their own circumstances present opportunities for pedagogy,[41] for teaching and learning about ourselves and others through connections that run from the past through the present. In particular, these stories raise important questions about the ways in which early market-based competition and the power assumed by the propertied minority shaped the substance and form of rural communities. In these stories we read the precursors to many of the circumstances facing rural towns today—corporate control, competition, and economic efficiency remain dominant as collective community efforts for social justice and freedom often take a back seat to the development of economic profit. These groups had broad popular support, and many read hope in their potential to protect farmers and rural communities from the vagaries of the market and the uncertainty agricultural work might bring. In addition to these community efforts, schooling and education contributed to the institutionalization of agrarian ideologies and values. Yet in what follows, as we consider the ways in which education served some but not all rural residents, particularly the children of the poor and tenant farmers, we'll also consider the implications of education that focused on developing a sense of place.

Reading School

By the late 1800s, Prairie Town had evolved into a town with wide muddy streets and a noted distinction among economic classes.[42] In time, wealthier families resided on the west side of town, dubbed "Piety Hill," a term attributable to the obvious wealth evident in the homes and the fact that it served as the locale for the only three English-speaking churches in the area.[43] Meanwhile, the east side of town, with its overcrowded school, was named "Poverty Hill." Children from the east side of town who were forced to attend school at Longfellows on the west side felt the brunt of the explicit class differences as "the Longfellow children weren't always so nice to those from the east side."[44]

The nearly seventy schools dispersed throughout the county in the early 1900s often have controversial location and relocation stories connected to them, many of which reflect the control property owners wielded in education matters. Similar to their control in community decisions, property owners also directed education activities to serve their dominant interests. Initially, many of the early schools were held in settlers' homes; however, as time passed, some of the large landowners donated land for the schools. Schools were sometimes moved after a series of town meetings; for instance, some documented relocations include moving a school from the northwest corner of a township to the southeast corner. Establishments of new districts, such as District 70 in 1919, were commonplace because of the great distance some of the children had to walk to school.

The physical placement of the school building was perhaps the biggest conflict in education, and decisions about where the schools would be located often resulted in long-lasting rifts within communities. Power structures, with those in the propertied minority providing a dominant voice, are evident in these struggles over schools:

> The often strange configurations in districts suggest that their evolution was a result of power dynamics rather than democratic action. The localism of midwestern rural ideology had great potential for exclusion and was likely more often used for this end than any other. Those who lived on the edge of certain districts may have simply been unlucky. Or they may have been tenant farmers, or immigrants, or members of a locally unpopular religious denomination.[45]

Students who lived a considerable distance from the township schools were often referred to as outside scholars. Paul Theobald noted that schools throughout the Midwest region had a variety of special policies for these students which were determined by local school boards and varied from charging tuition to denying admittance.

Language, ethnicity, and culture also contributed to the exclusiveness of these early communities. Prairie Town's earliest schools were mostly conducted in the native language of these isolated smaller communities as children learned to read, write, calculate numbers, and share the values and morals that were consistent with their forebears. It wasn't until the time of World War I that the county's German and Norwegian communities began to conduct school and religious services in the English language.[46] This change in language instruction was not due to the community's change in heart, but instead is attributable to planned policies at the federal and state level. The fact that so many retained their native language, rather than learn and use English, concerned leaders in the federal government and Minnesota. In fact, in 1918, the *Minneapolis Tribune* contained an article that stated:

> There is absolutely no need of perpetuating a Germany, or a Norway, or any other country in America. People have left there . . . because this land of opportunity will enable them to gain a position they never could have attained in their European home, and why, then, should that European country be held up to the detriment of America through the medium of the public school? . . . Pass a law prohibiting every language but American in our schools . . . then enforce it.[47]

Learning English wasn't necessary for the early settlers, primarily because store clerks and others with whom they conducted business or religious events spoke their own language. Some of the German settlements were particularly tight-knit, with many not learning English until they needed to leave the community. Few of the early immigrants had contact with other nationalities, and there was often distrust of those who were perceived to be different. Religious affiliation contributed further to the segregation of these early communities. However, by 1919, under pressure to Americanize its immigrants, Minnesota's state legislature enacted a law requiring English to be the medium of instruction in all public schools.[48] As such, schools became a tool used to reproduce exclusiveness.

Ultimately, the purpose of these early schools was to educate children in ways that would affirm their lives on the farm and prairie, and remain consistent with the traditions and value consensus of the early settlers' ethnic groups. Paul Theobald[49] observed that recitation was the most common pedagogical practice in rural midwestern schools during this time, and it is likely that Prairie Town's schools were no exception to this. There was an emphasis, through practices such as recitation, on maintaining the status quo, on keeping things as they were. This practice reflects broader goals of social maintenance and compliance with traditions.

Education about agricultural work has long been respected throughout Prairie Town, and from the time of the early settlers, education was considered a way to make farm life and agricultural work more efficient. This was perhaps most evident at the turn of the twentieth century when children who completed the eighth grade at their community schools could choose to attend Prairie Town's newly established Agricultural High School, housed on the grounds of what had previously been an Indian School for children of the nearby Sisseton-Wahpeton nation.[50] At the agricultural school, children could obtain an education during the off-season (between harvest and spring planting time) that would teach them more effective ways to manage their life on the farm. The Agricultural High School's curriculum, reflecting the gender biases of the time, emphasized farming for boys and home economics for girls.

The Agricultural School's commonly shared expectation was that once students completed their course of study they would return to their farms with new ideas and improved methods for agricultural and domestic work. The school did not disrupt the way of life for these rural families, but rather extended and enriched how they lived on their farms. Agricultural research was central to the work of the teachers in the school, as they experimented with diverse crops, crop rotation, soil, and animal research. The values of the agricultural school were similar to those of land grant institutions, many of which were newly established during this same time period. The emphasis of this education was to foster technicians, rather than to develop intellectuals, and the curriculum and research focused on the technical aspects of farming. The research was directed toward improving agricultural efficiency and quality, reflecting a sense of intradependence that was integral to the communities during this time. Paul Theobald explained:

> Intradependence speaks of dependence within a place, dependence on the land and dependence on the good will and wisdom of the people with whom the land is shared. The greater the intradependence, the greater the sense of community.[51]

In many respects, the agricultural school could serve the rural commitment to this intradependence, furthering a literacy that read the local community as a symbol of stability, encouraging young people to live well where they were. However, such instrumentalism could be considered an eventual factor in the shortcomings the community faced in terms of reinventing themselves. During the early days in Prairie Town, it was largely expected that children would stay close to their families and communities when they were adults, but this did little to help young people understand how to negotiate life in the local community in relation to the influences of broader society. For many, this value remains strong and is evidenced as those who live there today speak openly of their commitment to the town and their inability to imagine life elsewhere.

Not long after its establishment, Prairie Town's Agricultural High School closed, an occurrence that reflected societal tensions and misperceptions regarding agriculture and rural life. Prairie Town's establishment of a liberal arts college in place of the Agricultural High School likewise signaled a more significant change in some community members' hopes for the purposes of schooling and the growing dominance of school literacy (described in detail in the following chapter). But at the same time, resistance to the university reflected a desire by some to retain a rural, isolated way of life that had characterized the town since its founding in the late 1800s. While some in the community felt that education should not fundamentally change the children who attended the school (in other words, education should reinforce agrarian rural values and way of life in the community), others began to believe that post-secondary education would offer their children different and somehow better options that would take them away from the rural farms where they were raised. Farm families struggled with whether agriculture would be the best choice for their children, a struggle that was felt in other rural communities as well. As one farmer's son in Prairie Town explained:

> Originally it was our thought that you would [grow up to farm]. My Dad expected all three of us boys to farm, and now there's only one farming. And it was always thought that way. Well now it's, you know, the realization that you can't all farm. But at that time it was expected of you, and so, even though there was a farm crisis, there still was pretty much stability in the schools. But then after this all sunk in, then all of a sudden the amount of children coming into the schools declined rapidly and people moving out was a big deal. There was a migration.[52]

In addition to questions about the sustainability and viability of rural life, technological changes in agriculture began to make farming less labor intensive, requiring fewer hands to complete the work. Families began to have fewer children, and there were less opportunities to work as a laborer on a large farm. While perhaps an unintended consequence of technology, the increased ease with which farming was conducted resulted in the loss of jobs for many in the region. The unpredictable and often devastating life on the family farm was not widely considered the best option for the young people in the county.[53] The traditional rural literacy, which read value in education for living well where one was, began to shift toward educating children for life outside of Prairie Town and work away from the farm.

In addition to these efforts to preserve a particular way of rural life from within and across rural communities, there were likewise efforts to change it based on influences that were initiated from outside rural regions. One effort, the

Country Life Movement, was particularly concerned with rural outmigration, while the other, the Farm Bureau, hoped to help farmers increase production and efficiency. The Country Life Movement and the Farm Bureau read the solutions and possible results for "the rural problem" in different ways than grassroots organizations did. To them, outmigration and inefficient farming practices signalled a threat to the capitalist economy of the early part of this century, and they felt that experts could thwart this potential threat. To begin, we'll consider "the rural problem" as defined by the Country Life Movement—the outmigration of rural residents to urban areas.

Reading the "Rural Problem": The Country Life Movement

Outmigration of rural residents to urban or suburban areas is not a recent phenomenon, even though it continues to this day. German sociologist Ferdinand Tonnies[54] (1855-1936) noted the trend from rural communities toward urban, industrialized areas, and he distinguished between community (*gemeinschaft*) and society (*gesellschaft*) largely based on his own personal experience witnessing the compromises his rural province made in order to accommodate increased modernization. *Gemeinschaft* existed based on "the subjective will of the members"[55] and the "consciousness of belonging together and the affirmation of the condition of mutual dependence."[56] Tonnies characterized the community (*gemeinschaft*) as real, typically agriculturally based, organic, intimate, and rooted in old traditions and mores. Meanwhile, he contrasted this with society (*gesellschaft*), depicted as public life that was often mechanical, transitory, and superficial.[57] *Gesellschaft* lacked the element of shared feeling typical of *gemeinschaft* and was instead defined as a more objective, purposeful relationship, one Tonnies saw as typical of industrialized society.

Tonnies believed that *gemeinschaft* was stronger in rural areas, and consequently he felt there was much worth preserving in the rural community. These distinctions, while typological, are useful in helping to understand Prairie Town, even to this day, as the trend toward *gesellschaft* continues to threaten the security and viability of *gemeinschaft* in this and other small rural communities. Over time, Prairie Town's traditional rural values have been influenced by industrial or urban ideals, resulting in changes that could be most readily evidenced in the population movement from rural to urban/suburban centers. This movement toward *gesellschaft*, or urban society, is a marked trend that is typically attributable to industrialization and capitalism.[58] In other words, changes in the means of production, from agriculture to industry for example, are key factors in this shift. While some urban areas may have pockets with characteristics that resemble *gemeinschaft*, it is more likely that *gesellschaft* influences changes in small communities, rather than the other way around.

The influences from outside rural communities contribute in part to outmigration trends. Outmigration from rural regions, including Prairie Town, to other areas caused concern for those living outside rural communities as well. For some, America without rural and agriculturally based communities seemed antithetical to the principles of early democracy. Because of this, the Country Life movement began in the early 1900s out of urban concerns about rural life and institutions, as well as "the economic behavior and performance of farmers."[59] Due to an overarching concern that the flight to urban areas, particularly by "bright" young people, would leave rural communities devastated, Country Lifers sought to improve the social and cultural resources in rural areas. By 1908, President Theodore Roosevelt formed the Commission on Country Life to solve what came to be called the rural problem, defined as:

[O]ne of preserving "a race of men in the open country that, in the future as in the past, will be the stay and strength of the nation in time of war, and its guiding and controlling spirit in time of peace."[60]

The Country Life Movement held to the tenet that rural living needed to be a viable aspect of American society. Without it, American democracy would deteriorate. This group began efforts toward renewing rural communities with attempts to reform public education in rural areas, relying on the progressive educational philosophies of John Dewey and others. Drawing on progressive understandings of the experiential nature of learning, the Country Life Commission attempted to reform curriculum by proposing studies that were relevant to the lived experiences of rural youth. Country Lifers also attempted to broaden what they considered a narrow curriculum by inserting music and the arts to "make rural schools livelier and more interesting places."[61] They felt that education should be more than the technical processes forwarded through institutions like the Agricultural High School. In addition to these attempts at curricular reform, the Country Life Movement advocated for rural school consolidations. These consolidations took place at a neighborhood level, which meant that the numerous schools located throughout rural townships were encouraged to merge, ultimately resulting in different types of instruction that became increasingly homogenized in terms of both language and curriculum.

According to Paul Theobald,[62] the primary strength of the Country Life Movement was its attempts to tailor the school curriculum to local communities. But at the same time, the undertaking has been considered a concerted effort to move decision making and the "circumstances of American life out of the hands of the people themselves and into the hands of experts."[63] In spite of the commission's efforts, the rural "problem" has never been solved per se, at least as Country Lifers defined the problem, and many rural communities continue to struggle to this day with issues considered by this group nearly a century ago.[64]

Creating Expert Farmers: The Farm Bureau

Similar to the Country Life Movement, the Farm Bureau, first established in 1911 in Broome County, New York, funded county agents, typically experts from outside rural communities whose goals included educating farmers in scientific agricultural methods. These bureaus had ties to business and commercial organizations, including International Harvester and Sears.[65] The membership typically included wealthier farmers, business people, and experts from land-grant colleges. By 1919, the Farm Bureau became federated, and it worked with the United States Department of Agriculture and agricultural colleges to help farmers with marketing strategies that would "rationalize agriculture, stabilize prices, ally farmers to business, not labor, and destroy agrarian radicalism."[66]

In the early years, the Farm Bureau, with its capitalist interests, was opposed to cooperatives, and their agenda often ran against the collective and cooperative work that joined farm families and their communities. Further, the group reproduced patriarchal hierarchies as men and women's work were treated separately. Because men's work carried a higher status, membership in the bureau was limited to men only. In addition, the bureaus often "individualized the farm family by isolating the interests of each of its members."[67] Because the bureau encouraged businessmen to join the organization, it was criticized, particularly by the Farmers' Union, for placing business interests over those of farmers. In many ways, this organization could be viewed as a precursor to the corporate takeover of family farms that gave rise to agribusiness, and the farmers who joined forces with the bureau were certainly implicated in this trend. In other words, there hasn't been a sudden radical shift where agribusinesses consumed family farms; instead, there was an evolving trend that involved not only corporations and businesses, but farmers, politicians, and others who shared ideological beliefs concerning the role capitalism should play in American agriculture.

The close ties the Farm Bureau established among wealthy farmers, the federal government, and agricultural colleges were perceived to give them unfair advantage over other farm groups.[68] For example, farmers were typically required to join the Farm Bureau in order to obtain information and aid from the federal government. The Farmers' Union and other cooperative, grassroots groups criticized the bureau's slow political response to farmers' economic conditions.[69] The ideological and social division between the Farm Bureau and grassroots organizations was particularly evident in its efforts to represent farmers "without representing the diversity of the farm community."[70]In spite of this, by the time of World War II, the bureau became a powerful lobby for farm issues.[71]

The American Farm Bureau Federation (AFBF) is still in existence today,[72] and it still shares deep ideological differences with the National Farmers' Union. The AFBF's primary mission is to implement policies developed by members in over 2,800 county bureaus and to provide programs to improve the financial well-being and quality of life for farmers. With more than five million members throughout the United States and Puerto Rico, the AFBF is currently the nation's largest farm organization. Yet, the group is still criticized for many of the same reasons it received scrutiny in its early days. In 1997, the AFBF had two times as many members as there were farmers in the United States, and only 48 percent of American farmers were members of the AFBF. This indicates the large number of nonfarm memberships held by businessmen, many of whom are aligned with some of the nation's largest agribusinesses, as well as the automobile, oil, and pesticide industries.[73] By 2001, it was ranked the fifteenth most powerful lobbying group on Capitol Hill.[74] The legislation it supports is typically aligned politically with the far right, and forwards an agenda that institutionalizes racist policies, as well as policies that harm the environment and further disserve the poor and disenfranchised in this country.[75] Some examples of the far-right agendas the bureau and its state affiliates endorse include the Montana Farm Bureau, which lobbied for schools to teach creationism and for the state to ship convicted criminals to Mexico. The Maryland Farm Bureau supported establishing the state's official language as English, while the Texas Farm Bureau worked to repeal the state's minimum wage legislation and sought reductions in the food stamp and free and reduced lunch program throughout the state. The organization has supported a long list of legislation and policies that are harmful to the environment as they forward ultra-conservative agendas, many of which have no direct connection to farming.

As the Country Life Movement and the Farm Bureau's efforts indicate, change in rural communities occurred in complex ways, with different ideologies and different visions of the role rural communities should play in the United States. There were grassroots efforts, governmental efforts, and expert groups working to preserve and sustain rural life:

> Policymakers did not simply impose changes in agricultural production, nor did farm people merely resist these changes. Instead change came through an interactive process in which farm people adopted, adapted, and resisted new practices, and government policies both created new conditions and reacted to the choices and actions of farm people . . . many farm people blended the modern and the rural and were satisfied with the modified country way of life.[76]

Although the goals of these various groups may appear on the surface to be similar—to sustain rural American life—the ideologies that drove these changes differed. This is perhaps most obvious in the different approaches used by the Farmers' Union and the Farm Bureau—the former relying on grassroots efforts directed largely by socialist ideologies, while the latter relied on alliances with business, agricultural schools, and governmental agencies and conservative agendas. In addition to these efforts, there were ever-present societal influences from outside rural communities that shaped the ways in which people came to imagine how they might live together. Advances in technology, including radio, television, films, and the Internet, as well as improved travel and means for shipping goods have allowed rural communities to have more ready access to goods and services as those available in suburban and urban areas. As Caplow, Bahr, Chadwick, Hill, and Williamson noted:

> Change . . . is something flowing irresistibly from the outside world. Continuity is furnished locally. The outside world continuously proposes new ways of living and thinking. The local community steadfastly resists most of these suggestions and modifies those it adopts into conformity with its own customs.[77]

The trend toward *gesellschaft*, toward industrial society is evident not only in outmigration, but also in the ways that rural people both ideologically and materially bring society into their rural communities. After the time of World War II, this trend toward industrial society and the accompanying capitalist ideology heightened in ways that moved capitalism and eventually neoliberalism as the primary force behind decisions made in and for rural regions. As capitalist aims gained dominance, the socialist and collective efforts that had traditionally been part of rural Minnesota became increasingly marginalized. This trend will be considered in much more detail in the following chapter as we discuss neoliberal ideologies and literacies. Before moving to this, we'll close with a discussion of the ways in which traditional rural literacies, the reading of rural life with an eye toward the past, remain in Prairie Town.

Traditional Rural Literacies Today

The quote that opened this chapter reflects a traditional rural literacy, a traditional way of reading rural life that surfaces at various times in and among different individuals in Prairie Town. In this quote, which was part of an editorial in the local newspaper, the author yearns for times past and for young people to appreciate the landmarks that he reads as indicative of a different and somehow better time in Prairie Town's history. The places he noted symbolize to him a heroic time in the town's history, a time when men tamed a seemingly untamable land. As such, the author reads these symbols with a longing for the past and with a profound sense of loss because, as he characterized it, "only the hills" have remained the same. This sense of loss, based largely on an imagined and sometimes mythological past, offers a context through which one might find refuge from the complexities of the present, preventing individuals from working toward any realizable future. In other words, a selective, nostalgic remembering of the past in the hope to return life to an illusory status quo is a benign exercise in the sense that this goal can never truly be realized. This is not to suggest that remembrances and texts of the past are not important. Rather, it is to suggest that the *uses* of those remembrances make the difference between a significant sense of loss and the possibility for a radical reworking of a new and hopeful rural life.

In this chapter, we considered the dominant and often competing ideologies that shaped readings of rural communities in the early settlement days in rural Minnesota. In turn, to this day there are traditional readings of rural life that interpret the language, symbols, and rewritings of the past with a wistful nostalgia for the old days. The long-standing symbols of traditional rural communities—the land, the farms and families, schools, and community groups—have shaped the meaning of rural communities and the life of people who live there. Yet, there is a struggle that emerges in these texts and symbols among those who hope to control the meanings of rural life. In the early days in Prairie Town, the struggle was primarily manifest as an ideological struggle between those who read profit-making in the newly tilled black soil and those who read a sense of place and collective unity for generations of their families. The contradictions run deeper than differing ideologies as we realize that even among those who read collective action with hope, there was extensive exclusion of those who were of different ethnic, linguistic, economic, and/or cultural backgrounds. Similarly while some read value in the land and generational continuity, these values could be compromised as pressures to increase food production changed the meaning of agriculture for some farmers. Likewise, many valued education, but not education that would change the consciousness of individuals in ways that would elicit a different literacy or alternative reading of the world. Instead, education was expected to help them live well where they were. While many in rural communities were largely wary of the "outside experts" from groups like the Farm Bureau, some joined forces with them and in many ways contributed to the demise of their neighbors' livelihoods and rural communities. Groups such as the Country Lifers and Farm Bureau introduced different tensions as rural people struggled with resisting and/or adapting to the language these groups inserted into rural life. For the most part, these groups read rural communities as inadequate and inefficient, and their language proposed new ways for rural groups to live together.

As we'll see in subsequent chapters, ideological struggles remain in Prairie Town, surfacing in and among individuals and different Discourse groups that work to understand the relationship Prairie Town has to the outside world and its possibilities for the future. In other words, people read the signs and symbols of rural Prairie Town in different ways. Some, as we see in this chapter, have a language and a longing for the past, and the meanings they struggle over as they despair about their loss of the past are indicative of broader ideological struggles in our society. These struggles are inevitable as diverse individuals and groups come together to forge new and different Discourses and as some resist having their literacies marginalized by society's imposition of different values and ide-ologies. Although ideology is often riddled with contradictions, and as Stanley Aronowitz[78] reminds us, not completely predictive of people's beliefs, we see tensions and conflicts as the more traditional literacy competes for dominance with more contemporary, more dominant literacies (particularly those imbued with neoliberal ideologies, as we'll see in the next chapter).

Prairie Town built a new water tower in 1999, one that still proudly bears the name of the chief engineer of the St. Paul and Pacific Railroad. To some, the tower symbolized change and hope for the future, but it still retained elements of the past, at least through the stories behind the name. Just as glimpses of water towers keep us from becoming lost as we roam the prairie, so do glimpses of these stories. These stories help us to understand the traditional rural literacies in the community, and they open up possibilities for interrogating the past and re-considering the present. Before turning to these possibilities, we need to first understand the other literacies that circulate in and across Prairie Town's resi-dents. We'll continue by turning our attention to the influences of capitalism, particularly as it has given way to neoliberalism and globalization in contempo-rary Prairie Town, causing those who live there to read their rural life in somewhat different ways than the literacies influenced by agrarian republicanism, socialism, and early American capitalism.

Chapter 4
Neoliberalism and Rural Literacy

The key to both productivity and competitiveness is the skills for our people and our capacity to use highly educated and trained people to maximum advantage in the workplace. In fact, however, the guiding principle on which our educational and industrial systems have been built is profoundly different; this guiding principle, for long highly successful, is now outmoded, and harmful, and the time has come to change it.[1]

Prairie Town buzzed with excitement on April 22, 1999. A Burger King fast food restaurant opened on Main Street, and Michael, the boys, and I, along with many of our neighbors, became caught up in the event. After school and work were over, we paraded into the scrubbed clean restaurant, which smelled of Whoppers, French fries, and cleaning solutions, and filled ourselves with food we previously needed to drive at least forty-five minutes to eat. As we took in this new yet familiar experience, the children around us, including our own, slid on and off the slippery new seats, noisily playing with their new Kids' Meal toys as their once warm food remained relatively untouched. Michael commented later that he couldn't remember ever seeing so many people in one place in town (with the exception of the County Fair) since we had moved to Prairie Town nearly eight months before, an observation that seemed accurate to me. The anticipation of the new restaurant's arrival and the timing of the opening (at the onset of spring weather, just as the "mud season" was ending) must have brought people from throughout the county to experience this event.

Burger King's arrival in Prairie Town could be read in a variety of ways, each demonstrating the complexity of ideologies that drive each respective reading. For some in the community, Burger King[2] was read as a sign of the rural community's inevitable demise, which was read differently by two different groups. For those who wanted to preserve the "ruralness" of the community, such a restaurant was read as evidence that the community was giving in to corporate America. It brought in outside culture and ideals in ways that not everyone appreciated, not just through the movie promotions and other mainstream advertisements, but also through its promotion of values that some considered contrary to rural life. Burger King wasn't "local" in the sense that the restaurant, its values, or even its food came from the community, and as such, it raised questions about which businesses should be supported in Prairie Town and consequently which should not. For some, having a local family open a restaurant in the former Hardee's building would have been more ideal.

A second group that read the rural community's demise in Burger King's arrival recognized neoliberalism's encroachment in yet another realm of rural life. Neoliberalism's emphasis on the economic at the expense of the social meant that standardization of products and consumerism were given primacy over any expressed concerns about promoting local goods and services. Those who recognized neoliberal influences in Burger King's arrival did not expect to return the community to the past as more traditional groups did. Instead, these individuals wanted to protect it from a future that would either subject the community to heightened expectations for capitalist production or would see its demise when the community was not able or willing to become normalized in ways that other towns and suburbs were.

Others read Burger King's opening only with hopefulness in mind. In the new restaurant, they read signs that the community was doing fine, in spite of reports of the town's economic decline, and they read the possibility for their community to stabilize and be like other towns. Those who readily welcomed the Burger King thought primarily of the jobs it would offer (even though the county had more jobs than workers), the convenience it would bring, and the "modernity" of the restaurant.

Because neoliberalism is a dominant ideology in today's society, often viewed as natural and self-evident, many read the Burger King with a mixture of these positions. They may have been excited to see the restaurant fill the empty space on Main Street. There were quite a number of empty buildings on Main Street, and Burger King's presence offered hope that this trend could be reversed. Having a Burger King in town seemed refreshing for those who hoped Prairie Town could have some of the same amenities that other communities had. While they may have preferred a locally owned and operated restaurant rather than a franchise, they did not seem to question its implications in the same way those critical of neoliberalism did. Although the town housed several franchised restaurants, including a McDonald's, a Pizza Hut, a Pizza Ranch, and a Taco John's, the Burger King seemed to boost morale for those who wanted to have at least the *appearance* of choice, for those who wanted to "have it your way."[3] For many in the community, Burger King's opening was read as a sign of progress. In spite of ever-present concern about outmigration from the community and a dwindling population, the Burger King served to contradict a sense that the town was deteriorating beyond rescue, and instead signaled hope for the future. It conveyed, at least to some, a sense that the town was surviving, a characteristic that could appeal to those who might consider visiting or moving into the community. It is particularly difficult to convince potential newcomers to move into town if Main Street is empty. It is this reading of rural life—a reading that silently subscribes to neoliberalism as an ideal for rural communities—that will be interrogated in this chapter as we slow down the values and consequences neoliberalism brings to rural towns.

Burger King's arrival in Prairie Town illustrates some of the tensions rural communities have faced, particularly over the past fifty years. By the end of World War II, societal and economic changes that emphasized industry over agriculture, an ever-growing corporate culture, and the gravitation of rural residents to urban areas and ideals largely worked to redefine rural communities. The traditional rural literacy, which read value in agricultural work, a homogenous community, and a sense of place, likewise changed as rural people attended to the signs of rural life differently and agrarian ideologies were no longer seen as adequate to meet the needs of an industrialized society. By the end of the century, neoliberalism was a hegemonic ideology.[4] Neoliberalism's key values infiltrated economic and political interactions throughout the world and were increasingly adopted by the public at large. During this time, neoliberalism influenced international economic groups, particularly the International Monetary Fund (IMF) and the World Bank. Pannu explained:

> The promotion [of neoliberalism] is effected through the well-coordinated set of macroeconomic stablization and structural adjustment policies of the supranatural institutions such as the IMF and World Bank. The IMF demands adoption and insists on the application of these macroeconomic policies by a large number of Third World debtor states, policies that bear the unmistakable imprint of neoliberalism. Further the mechanisms used to secure compliance approach market colonialism. Similarly the World Bank, which is also controlled by the major capitalist states, uses its enormous financial power, delicately fused with technocratically anointed and bureaucratically produced knowledge, to "persuade" in myriad ways developing country ruling elites to follow policies that are consistent with and rooted in economic liberalism.[5]

At an international level, neoliberalism's influence rapidly moved countries, whether they liked it or not, toward globalization and a market economy.[6] These policies influenced trade, agriculture, employment, and the quality of life in the United States and elsewhere.

In rural Prairie Town, those who read the community with neoliberal ideologies in mind found many shortcomings in their rural way of life. The town and rural life seemed inefficient and often poorly equipped to meet the needs for its citizens in a changing global economy. Because neoliberalism as an ideology frames explanations of social issues in economic terms, rural poverty and the labor and wage issues endemic to many rural communities were defined as social issues that could be solved with jobs and better pay.[7] Similarly, family farms were considered inadequate because they couldn't turn a profit in the same way large scale and corporate farms could. To neoliberals, small farms were a way of the past, and because they weren't economically viable in relation to their big business counterparts, there was no reason to expect them to sustain a farmer's existence. These messages to rural communities—namely that their way of life was no longer adequate, particularly given the needs of the global economy—caused some living in these communities to read rural life differently. The signs that once indicated hope for rural people (particularly the potential for intergenerational continuity and intradependence) became read as signs of the past, the hope for which would only lead to despair. As such, education for place was no longer deemed efficient, and education instead became a vehicle for leaving rural communities. Local literacies and values became marginalized as education was increasingly standardized to meet the claim that schools could serve the demands of the global workforce.[8] At the same time, community became less stable, due in part to what Pierre Bourdieu called a state of "precarite":

> [I]nsecurity of social standing, uncertainty about the future of one's livelihood and the overwhelming feeling of "no grip on the present"—combine into an incapacity to make plans and to act on them . . . the chances of resistance to the moves of power-holders, and particularly of steady, organized and solidary resistance, are minimal—virtually non-existent.[9]

"The rural," at least as it was defined by more traditional agrarian and socialist ideologies, became increasingly perceived as unstable, substandard, and consequently undesirable.[10]

This chapter offers a discussion of the changes in rural communities that occurred over the latter half of the twentieth century, largely due to capitalism's hegemonic influence and, consequently, the ways in which these changes have been read by rural residents. While the early days in Prairie Town saw struggles over the meaning of rural life in relation to competing ideologies (i.e., capitalism, socialism, and agrarianism), the last fifty years in particular witnessed struggles for survival that reflected the increasing dominance of capitalist ideologies. These ideologies measured individuals' worth based on their economic wealth, rather than social responsibilities or efforts. Socialist ideals and agrarianism were marginalized as government policies and corporate trends valued profit over people,[11] forcing farmers and other businesses to get big or get out. Consequently, as capitalism gave way to neoliberalism, particularly throughout the 1980s and 1990s, the ways in which some rural people read the texts and signs of farm and land, community, and education changed. This chapter captures some of those changes as we continue to discuss the three themes begun in chapter three (farm and land, community, and education), and the ways in which they were read in rural Prairie Town. To begin, we'll consider the changes that occurred as farm and land became read through a language of efficiency, mass production, commodification, and profit.

Reading Farm and Land

Food sold at Burger King doesn't come directly from Prairie Town farms. Instead, its products are purchased through contracts with various food-processing plants, including Iowa Beef Processors (IBP) and other purveyors that ship their products throughout the nation, companies that in turn have contracts with farmers. Like most franchised restaurants, Burger King offers uniformity in its menu options, efficiency in food production, and relatively low and similar prices throughout the United States and abroad. For this reason, a Whopper in upstate New York looks and tastes just like a Whopper in Fargo, North Dakota, and the dining experience is relatively constant across place as employees typically have the same uniforms nationwide and stores have the same design, color schemes, and decorations. As Americans, we seem to expect this consistency as we seek out familiar restaurants, even when we travel to unfamiliar destinations.

Since the 1950s, contracts between farmers and food industries have increasingly driven the food production business.[12] Farmers traditionally produced food for self-sustenance and local consumption, but the expanding commercialization of the food industry, coupled with technological changes and improved shipping and transportation methods, brought changes in agreements, or contracts, between farmers and food corporations. Basically, contracts are "agreements between farmers and companies or other farmers that specify conditions of production and/or marketing of an agricultural product. By combining market functions, contracting can reduce industry participants' exposure to risk."[13] Ordinarily, there are two types of contracts: marketing and production. Marketing contracts typically establish the price or pricing mechanism for a crop or commodity before harvest, while production contracts are detailed specifications of what the contractor will provide, when they will provide it, and what the compensation for the farmer will be. Sometimes a farmer will contract with other farmers to complete a particular stage of production, particularly in livestock raising, allowing the farmer who is the contractor to specialize in another stage.

While the use of contracts in farming is controversial, those who endorse it suggest that it allows farmers to rapidly expand their operations, and they propose that less debt and fewer financial risks accompany such expansion.[14] Much like the Fordist model of production that infiltrated the meat-packing industry in the 1970s, contracts compartmentalize farming processes, and farmers become responsible for narrower aspects of agricultural work. One farmer's wife in Prairie Town explained:

> The people that farm around [Prairie Town] I think now tend to be the larger families and not just the little [ones]. You know, we used to have 200 acres and [we were a] little, you know, diversified to different livestock. Now it isn't quite like that. People are almost specialized . . . and they farm greater amounts of land. . . . I've lived on a farm for thirty years. When we first started out I know that we didn't farm as much land and I . . . know we had chickens, and

cattle, and hogs, and now we have maybe four, five times as much land and we have just cattle. . . . Many farms have done that, it seems to me. We've either got hog farmers, cattle farmers, chicken farmers, or whatever the case might be, but you just have the one operation.[15]

It was not uncommon for farmers in Prairie Town to have contracts with Land o' Lakes and other major food industries.

According to the U.S. Department of Agriculture,[16] farmers typically enter into contracts because they offer income stability and help with the management of cash flow (for example, payments to farmers may extend over the course of a year or more). Further, contracts are believed to offer some measure of market security, along with increased access to capital for farmers, primarily because the contractor supplies the means for production. Contracts are also believed to improve the efficiency of farm operations.

Food processors, like Tyson, Hanover Foods, and others, typically enter into contracts because they can gain greater control of the supply, and they can improve response to consumer demands. Contracts are particularly appealing to food processors that desire uniformity and predictability, and the increased efficiency and control of production allow them to expand and diversify. Vertical integration, a process whereby integrators control consecutive states of the food production system as well as the inputs into this system, is increasingly owned and controlled by a single company.[17] For example, Tyson Foods breeds the parent stock for their chickens, produces the hatching eggs (typically through a contract), hatches the eggs, and then contracts with growers to raise the chickens. Meanwhile, vertical coordination, the "synchronizing of product transfer from one stage of production to the next," coupled with contracts and vertical integration, is beginning to replace what was once called open-market coordination.[18]

Those who oppose contracts are concerned about the growing disparity in bargaining power between contractors and producers, a relationship that puts farmers in jeopardy of being abused by large corporations. There is also concern about the environmental consequences of increasingly centralized food production, particularly as it pertains to large animal feeding facilities and animal waste management control. Further, the increasing concentration of production is suspected to contribute to a loss of autonomy and independence for farmers and an increasing homogenization of food in the country. Senator Chuck Grassley of Iowa, among others, has expressed concern that larger farmers and agribusinesses, those in control of agricultural contracts, are dominating the market and dictating the terms and prices offered in contracts. Further, there is growing sentiment that such control is not being taken into account in anti-trust laws, anti-trust investigations, and other similar legal issues. The U.S. government has legislation relating to contracts with farmers; however, the government's policies have tended to support agribusiness and large corporations rather than small farmers.[19]

Where farmers once read their role in agriculture in ways that tempered socialist and agrarian ideologies against the capitalist ideals that captured the imagination of a young American democracy, they now tended to read their role primarily through a capitalist language of markets, mass production, efficiency, and uniformity in mind. It wasn't uncommon to see an old "American made"[20] pickup truck driving through Prairie Town with a sticker proudly proclaiming "I feed the world" plastered to its back bumper. The expectations for this new type of farming that fed the world rather than local communities employed a new literacy that read farming as a commodity rather than a way of life, constituting it through a language imbued with capitalist principles. One consequence of this highly commodified approach to farming was that it drove many into debt as they purchased equipment and other means to increase production and capacity. This in turn increased disparities between large- and small-scale farmers, between the rich and poor, increasingly driving smaller farmers out of business.

The contradictions between the new language of farming, particularly that embodied a language of mass production, and the more traditional expectations that constituted the founding of these farms, the traditional agrarian ideologies, caused personal agony for many farmers. Farms were no longer read as a sign of individual responsibility within a collective community, and they were no longer read as essential to local self-sustenance. Instead, they were read as a cog in a larger production wheel. In other words, farmers read their experiences, not against the local needs and expectations of their community, but rather against the expectations contractors and agribusinesses demanded. These expectations were sometimes in conflict with local well-being, particularly as larger and fewer farms contributed to the decline of rural communities and the pollution in rural lands and waters. Heightened competition among larger farmers and the federal government's tendency to reward larger-scale farms through formulas that were production-based has contributed to economic growth and expansion among corporate farms, simultaneously working to move agriculture away from traditional agrarian ideals toward industrial and capitalistic realms.

Changes in capitalist production of the food industry that influenced rural readings of farm and land also influenced changes in readings of rural communities. Where there was once the potential to bring farmers together to negotiate their collective survival through local efforts of the Farmers' Alliance, the Non-Partisan League, and other similar groups, there now seemed to be more fragmentation in rural communities as competition increased, as small farms and businesses went out of business, and as people migrated from rural communities to suburban and urban areas in search of jobs. People began to read the local community as unstable, rather than as a place of security. In the next section, we'll consider these trends and the influence neoliberalism had on rural communities.

Reading Community

When sociologist Ferdinand Tonnies characterized rural communities as *gemeinschaft*, inviting the rural community's "return from the exile to which it had been banished during the modern crusade against . . . narrowing of horizons and nurturing of superstition,"[21] he pointed out that rural communities inherently had a shared understanding by all its members. As sociologist Zygmunt Bauman pointed out, Tonnies' *gemeinschaft* is different from present-day understanding of consensus among a community of people, different from an agreement that involved compromises and negotiations. Instead *gemeinschaft's* shared understanding served as a testament to the inherent ideological homogeneity that characterized rural communities. With increased communication, transportation, and other technological advances, communities became diverse both ideologically, as ideas and values from society were incorporated into communities, and culturally and ethnically. As such, shared understandings could only give way to consensus building, to debate over the ways in which people would come to live together. As Bauman characterized it:

> From now on, all homogeneity must be "hand-picked" from a tangled mass of variety through selection, separation and exclusion; all unity needs to be *made*; concord "artificially produced" is the sole form of unity available. Community understanding can only be an *achievement*, attained (if at all) at the end of a long and tortuous labour of argument and persuasion and in strenuous competition with an indefinite number of other potentialities—all vying for attention and each promising a better (more correct, more effective, or more pleasurable) assortment of life tasks and solutions for life problems.[22]

Over the latter half of the twentieth century, the struggle for community understanding and solutions for life problems became increasingly complicated, particularly as trends toward centralized governance, official language policies, and standardized education took hold, shifting the potential for real debate into the hands of a few. Modern capitalism, which separated business from the household, likewise freed livelihoods from "the web of moral and emotional, family and neighborly bonds."[23] At the same time, enlightenment ideals increasingly cast the local as backward, promoting nation building as a process of unifying diverse ways of life into one unified whole. In this way, communities, whether local or ethnic, in a nationalist sense became "prime suspects and the principal enemies."[24] Assimilation was key, with dominant groups directing the nation-building process:

> The choice of fate was not always left to the communities. The decision as to who was and who was not fit for assimilation (and conversely, who was bound to be excluded and prevented from contaminating the national body and sapping the sovereignty of the nation-state) was for the dominant majority, not for the dominated minorities, to take.[25]

By the end of the twentieth century, community was increasingly cast in neoliberal terms, a trend that heightened efforts toward assimilation of values and ways of life. This hegemonic ideology expected "them" (the economically poor, the ethnic minority, the immigrant) to become more like "us" (the middle class, Eurocentric, native-born Americans), particularly in terms of shared values and shared understandings of what it meant to be an American citizen. As President Clinton once explained:

> I have followed a very simple strategy. I think it's the basic American bargain—opportunity for all/responsibility from all, and then telling every single person if you will be responsible, if you will seize your opportunity, if you believe in the Constitution, the Declaration of Independence, and the Bill of Rights, you don't have to tell us anything else. We don't care what your race is, we don't care what your religion is, we don't care where you started out in life. If you're willing to work hard and share our values, we'll join arm and arm with you and walk together into the future. You're part of our America.[26]

Neoliberals became increasingly concerned about what they saw as the decline of community, a phenomenon they cast in mainstream (i.e., white middle class) terms. They attributed this so-called decline to the deterioration of key institutions, such as universal military service and public schools, and to political differences between Republican and Democratic parties that have failed to contribute to a sense of community.[27] One way neoliberals hoped to restore community values in the United States was through a "communitarian ideology with broad popular appeal."[28] However, this espoused goal often translated into a hidden agenda that worked to normalize the constituents of any given community. In other words, there is a particular narrowness to the neoliberal vision of freedom and equality, a vision that seeks conformity to a specific, privatized view of democracy that works to protect the wealth and well-being of those who hold power in the United States.[29]

At the same time, market forces worked to normalize and pull attention away from the more formidable and challenging issues in our society, such as racism, poverty, and oppression. Instead of opening up possibilities to understand and negotiate differences, differences were cast as deviant, particularly for those who did not obtain material wealth. Attention to the market created a general failure to acknowledge the societal obstacles and social injustices that prevented some from gaining security of standing, let alone economic wealth (including the lack of living wage for a large percentage of American workers, the need for universal health care, and a federal income tax system that is weighted to disproportionately favor the wealthy, to name a few). Likewise, there was failure to acknowledge that some individuals and groups, including many who choose to live in rural communities, measure success in terms that are other than economic. This position, that success and community can be constituted around causes that are other than economic, runs contrary to many neoliberals, including Clinton's former labor secretary Robert Reich, who casts the community as a commodity, emphasizing wealth as the key factor in joining individuals. He explained:

> You pick a community for exactly what you want from it. As with other aspects of your new life, you shop for the best aspects you can afford. Because exit is so easy and the benefits are so targeted, these new communities don't require nearly so much commitment as the old did, nor do they offer the same security

to members who might need to depend on one another in a pinch. . . . Given the range of choice and the ease of switching, we're sorting ourselves into communities of people with roughly the same incomes, the same abilities, the same risks, and the same needs. Where we live has more to do with how much we earn than ever before.[30]

Those who once read community as a collective struggle united around shared values that included cultural and ethnic commitments, religious affiliation, and other goals, likely find no connection to the community as defined by neoliberals. Of course Reich's views only reflect the sentiments of those who are "travelers" in this new economy—those like Reich who can move easily from place to place, choosing where they want to live and work. For the vast majority of the population, those who are "vagabonds" and are either forced to remain where they are or must move from place to place as jobs, political events, or natural catastrophes dictate, there are no real choices,[31] in spite of neoliberal assurances of such.

Neoliberalism promises rewards to those who share common values— "America is a land of opportunity if you do as we say."[32] In other words, those who will work and live in particular ways are expected to achieve financial success for themselves and for the country.[33] However, this overarching view of material success does not always match with the values of rural communities, many of which have eschewed financial gain in search of different values and lifestyles,[34] employing different literacies that read the world in ways that are different from neoliberals. Rather than looking for a community that would bring them financial gain, some in rural communities looked for communities that would accept their hope to sustain their own existence as well as their ability to define and control their own lives. The tensions between neoliberal expectations for community and the more traditional agrarian influences resulted in Prairie Town's officials struggle with striking a balance between helping the town survive and what they feared would be compromising the more traditional values of rural life.[35] The town and its people had a history of resisting big business, particularly agribusiness and larger industries because of the potential changes (which town members expected would be mostly negative) they would bring to the community, and they often struggled with the changes ethnic and cultural diversity would bring. This resistance, coupled with the resistance to outsiders,[36] made the promotion of industry and tourism in the area seem a less likely solution for the community's survival. Instead, other options needed to be formulated, different languages needed to be employed, and new ways of reading rural life needed to be developed.[37]

Next to economic development, education has been considered by many to be the primary vehicle for the so-called renewal of rural communities,[38] and success in education leading to success in the job market is another promise commonplace in neoliberal rhetoric. In Prairie Town, the end of World War II marked a time of economic and societal change that provided an impetus for what would eventually materialize as neoliberalism becoming the dominant ideology. In education, this Discourse held that mastery of academic curriculum and school knowledge was necessary and would lead to later success in life away from this community. This phenomenon has become increasingly common in rural areas, resulting in significant consequences:

> In many rural communities, schools have become vehicles for educating people to leave, fulfilling the prophecy that these places are doomed to poverty, decline, and despair. They have cooked their own goose.[39]

Just as the promise of work doesn't guarantee that jobs will be well-paying or meet living wage requirements, the promise of particular types of education (i.e., those increasingly defined through the language of standards and high stakes testing) does not guarantee an individual or a community any measure of success. As we'll see in what follows, this is evident in Prairie Town which, like many rural communities, struggles with the purposes, values, and end results of the education it provides its young people.

Reading School

Neoliberalism influenced public education by narrowing its purpose, beginning with the ability to read, toward curricula they expected would secure American economic success in the new global marketplace.[40] For many schools across the nation, this heightened emphasis on the economy manifests itself through an education success equation that proposed students were human capital and would need to be life-long learners in order to succeed economically in an ever unpredictable job market.[41] One result was an increased emphasis on accountability through standardized curricula and high stakes testing.[42] Public education was held up as a way to equalize the playing field across racial, cultural, and economic differences, in spite of increasing evidence that high stakes accountability perpetuated differences.[43] These continuing disparities resulted in higher dropout rates among limited English proficient and minority students, differentiated resources, particularly for urban and rural schools,[44] and other infrastructure and human disparities.[45] For those who held fast and true to the tenets of neoliberalism, there was a belief that sharing in the same values and same goals would lead to the American dream.[46]

Rural towns in the Midwest typically have schools Paul Nachtigal[47] has described as "traditional Middle America" schools, places where academic achievement tends to be above average, graduation rates are high, and athletic activities play a central role. In many ways, Garrison Keilor's talk of Lake Wobegon, where all students are above average, rings true in the Prairie Town School District where 1,215 students attend either the elementary school or the high school. In the 1999-2000 school year, 90 percent of the eighth grade students passed the Minnesota Comprehensive Assessments[48] in Reading the first time they took it, while 80 percent passed the Math portion of the same test on their first attempt. Further, county data indicates that less than 1 percent of the school population failed to graduate from high school, and fully 95 percent of the school population was considered "college bound." In addition, nearly 800 students participated in an extracurricular sport at some time during the academic year,[49] and these students received much support from the community in terms of attendance at games and financial assistance through fundraising activities. By all accounts, the school in Prairie Town seemed to be doing well for its students. But changes loomed at the end of the 1990s at the state's new graduation standards, high stakes testing, and budget cuts introduced new circumstances for educators, parents, and students alike. These changes should be read against the context of neoliberal influences, as the standards movement, the emphasis on accountability and efficiency, were commonplace as neoliberalism became a dominant ideology.

Parents and teachers were acutely aware of the changes facing the district. Because of this, they engaged in a series of town meetings held during the 1999-2000 academic year. As community members met to discuss the future of the school in light of declining enrollments and infrastructure needs, they expressed hope that their students would receive an education that included traditional, core academic subject areas (mathematics, English, science, social studies), the arts and music, language, physical fitness, and technology. In fact, a new vision statement for the district, created during these meetings, articulated only the positive qualities of life in a *small town*. It emphasized that the school should "capitalize on the unique opportunities that a small community can provide, particularly the positive sense of belonging and family that is important in small communities."[50] Missing was any mention of the positive qualities of *rural* life or agricultural work, nor did there appear to be a place for children to read value in the local community. Just as the arrival of Burger King failed to engage any language to critique the status quo, the planning for the school district fell short of disrupting the norms the community came to expect for its school's ability to export students. In other words, parents and teachers seemed preoccupied with ensuring their children would be ready to leave the community in the future, further contributing to the town's demise. As we turn our attention toward a discussion of the primary values of neoliberalism as they were realized in Prairie Town's school,[51] we'll consider three issues: standardization, a heightened accountability for schools, and the assumption of equal opportunity through education.

Standardization of Education

Throughout the late 1980s and 1990s, education became increasingly standardized as groups, such as the New Standards Project,[52] and states, with the exception of Iowa, worked to develop and implement standards for public school students to meet.[53] With the premise that high standards would improve student learning came at least two implicit assumptions about schools: first, that conditions for teaching are standard and adequate; and second, that the conditions for learning, including adequate resources, are standard. Yet in Prairie Town, as in many other schools throughout the nation, this was not always the case.

By 1998, Prairie Town School was required to ensure that students would meet state established standards, called the Profile of Learning, and pass the state's new basic skills tests, required for graduation. The ten areas of learning outlined in the profile included: read, listen and view; write and speak; arts and literature; mathematics applications; scientific applications; people and cultures; decision making; resource management; and world languages. Although on the surface these ten learning areas may seem to reflect a more liberal view of education, the underlying purpose was to better prepare children for the workforce and the global economy.[54]

As the state outlined the standards and set the requirements, they expected local districts to determine how to best meet the standards.[55] To ensure teachers were meeting requirements, they required districts to submit their teaching plans, called performance packages, for review. These performance packages would provide students opportunities to demonstrate their progress toward the state goals. Initially high school graduates were required to complete twenty-eight of these packages; after the first year of implementation, the number was decreased to twenty. To help with this, the state offered performance packages as models schools could implement, provided graduation standard technicians[56] to assist with these efforts, and then required districts to submit their own packages to the state for review before teachers could implement their plans.

Throughout this process of implementing the new requirements, one difference between Prairie Town and most other schools was that the district served as a pilot site before the standards were mandated. Most teachers attributed this decision to the fact that the district would receive more state monies if they piloted the standards. Serving as a pilot site happened often in the district, as declining enrollments coupled with the state's per pupil funding formula[57] made the district more vulnerable to new reforms as the teachers and administration felt a need to generate revenues for the school in as many ways as they could. However, already short on time, resources, and personnel, the teachers often felt frustrated and susceptible to the whims of the state administration as they piloted various programs. One teacher explained:

> We were a pilot site, [but] as a pilot site it's been frustrating. So frustrating . . . there have been so many changes that have already occurred and so we had to get on board and we were doing it one way . . . and then [the state] would come in, you know, after the session, and they would say, no you're going to do it this way.[58]

Another teacher shared a similar story:

> Here, well, we've spent a lot of time writing and rewriting [performance packages], but I guess it seems that [Prairie Town] has been a district that kind of jumps onto things right away. So we got grant money for [piloting the standards], so we had the money to spend.[59]

In addition to feeling demoralized by the need to be a pilot site, the teachers also lived with the uncertainty of losing their jobs. One teacher explained:

Well, declining enrollment. I guess I have to think about that . . . but I don't.
But I probably should . . . because we settled our contract last night, and it was
stated at that point that there just isn't money available because the students
aren't here, and that we're going to have major cuts. Well, I am the second to
the bottom on the seniority list in our elementary school. . . . I asked [the prin-
cipal] this morning, you know, what is the deal? And he said, major cuts. So, I
guess it is possible that I could lose my job because of it.[60]

The situations facing teachers in Prairie Town could be considered demor-
alizing at best, and further complicated by dwindling resources in the district. As
Minnesota's legislature demanded more production, mandating standardization
of programs and testing emphasizing academic learning directed toward college
preparation,[61] there was less money available for the teachers. Those teaching in
Prairie Town noted the dire circumstances they faced. One teacher explained:

I think we're so limited even with multiple copy books and updating those. And
literature books all around. I don't know. I just think, you know, in your bigger
school, you just have more money. You've got a lot more spending going on . .
we have an old school and old desks and I don't have enough books even to
teach my kids social studies.[62]

Similarly, Prairie Town's elementary school librarian reported having one-
half less budget money than she did when she began working for the district in
the 1970s. With rising costs for books, book repair, and equipment, she could
purchase significantly fewer texts for the school.

[W]ith declining enrollment, [my budget is] being cut again. With books . . .
averaging out like 16 to 17 dollars even for a picture book, trying to work
within that budget and still keep books that interest the kids, but yet working
with the faculty so that they have reference or resource books that they can pull
to take to their classroom when they're doing things, it's hard to be all things to
everybody. . . . And then with the usage . . . there's wear and tear you know,
and we used to send books to the bindery. We can't afford to do that any more.
Just to replace books that have been damaged or lost, it's really almost impossible. . . . People expect certain services, and once they're taken away, will it
ever be reinstated? Will you ever get books back that you've lost? . . . that not
only affects the books and other services, but it's the equipment as it ages, the
overheads, the tape recorders. We've already cut back on cassette tapes that we
used to give the teachers if they needed them. The video tapes . . . we've
dropped that. We just keep dropping services little by little by little.[63]

The state attempted to equitably fund its public schools by using a per pupil
formula, but as districts faced declining enrollments, it became increasingly difficult for them to adjust their local tax base to compensate for the loss in revenue. The discrepancy in resources and materials between wealthier school districts, schools that were able to balance the state's per pupil funding equation
against a different tax base than that in Prairie Town, coupled with the expectation that outputs in student learning should be increased, caused some to argue

for increases in the "economies of scale" in the region by consolidating the schools. In fact, Minnesota had a policy in place to encourage such consolidations.[64] However, Prairie Town and many neighboring communities resisted this trend, largely due to a belief that once the school was gone from the community, the community would decline beyond repair.[65] Further, they watched carefully throughout the 1980s as "cornfield schools," consolidated schools that were placed geographically in the middle of a few communities, were built. Often students were bussed great distances to attend these schools, and they did little to unite communities. They also incurred high costs due to the services (water, sewer, electrical, Internet, etc.) that needed to be directed out of town to the fields where these schools were located. Consolidation was the last choice for Prairie Town and many communities.

Prairie Town's teachers, several of whom won state recognition through Minnesota Teacher of the Year nominations and other national and internatonal awards (including one from NASA and another from World School Japan), clearly had the potential and hope to offer creative and worthwhile educational experiences for their students that extended above and beyond the required mandates from the state. However, their creative work was increasingly marginalized as the state expected teachers' efforts to be directed toward particular standards that may or may not have corresponded with the school's curriculum and/or the teachers' talents and interests. Certainly some teachers needed to justify the teaching of particular units of study that weren't easily matched with the state requirements. One teacher who had won awards from NASA's Space Program and loved to share his passion for outer space with students explained how he was still able to work in his outer space unit, even though it didn't fit easily with the state standards:

> [L]uckily we pushed our science standard to the sixth grade, so we're getting my space stuff in, not even through the science standard. I'm getting it in through [the] inquiry [standard] and through [the] reading [standard]. [66]

The state standards, reinforcing neoliberalism's dominance, worked to deskill[67] teachers, attempting to strip away the intellectual aspects of their work as they became "standards technicians." At the same time, the standards had the potential to remove educational experiences, or at least limit opportunities for experiences, that would be unique to local communities.

The standards movement in Minnesota and other states occurred within a context of neoliberal federal expectations that at least two years of postsecondary education should be the norm,[68] and many of the standards were developed with this ideal in mind. Children who had aspirations that did not require two years of postsecondary education were marginalized, as were their programs. For example, a vocational education teacher at Prairie Town High School spoke publicly at a town meeting regarding the outdated equipment and technology that was available for his program and students. What had once been a well-respected cabinetmaking program was in jeopardy due to obsolete equipment and limited resources. The teacher received little financial or moral support in a school that was already struggling financially and hoping to invest more dollars in its technology for academic rather than vocational programs. This same teacher worked with the Future Farmers of America group at the high school, and he likewise noted the lack of attention and status given to the students who participated in this program. He asked for community acknowledgement and media attention (through the local newspaper and a small radio station) to credit the accomplishments of these students, who he felt received less accolades than their peers in the athletic and academic clubs in the school. Neoliberalism's influence allowed little room for reading value in the local and the rural aspects of Prairie Town; in other words, the school, generally speaking, had little value for local literacies.

The increasing emphasis on school success as it leads to postsecondary education is a phenomenon that reflects the status quo in Prairie Town and other communities. As journalist Nicholas Lemann[69] observed:

> Here is what American society looks like today. A thick line runs through the country, with people who have been to college on one side of it and people who haven't on the other. This line gets brighter all the time. Whether a person is on one side of the line or the other is now more indicative of income, of attitudes, and of political behavior than any other line one might draw: region, race, age, religion, sex, class. As people plan their lives and their children's lives, higher education is the main focus of their aspirations (and the possibility of getting into the elite end of higher education is the focus of their very dearest aspirations). A test of one narrow quality, the ability to perform well in school, stands firmly athwart the path to success. Those who don't have that ability will have much less chance than those who do to display their other talents later.

It has become part of the culture of schooling that public education should lead to higher education, and those who are either unwilling or unable to pursue a college degree are less likely to be considered successful in the new economy. Because so many of the high school students continue on to higher education when they graduate from Prairie Town High School, most young people leave the area upon graduation.[70] This trend, commonplace in other rural communities, has significant social and economic implications for those who remain:

> Effective rural schools typically "export" their best "products," leaving behind families and communities that often are or ought to be anxious or ambivalent about school success and school completion. . . . National efforts to improve the life chances of rural at-risk children ought to better recognize and better support rural schools. . . . [The schools] are not the cause of economic decline in rural places. Rather, they are the institutions that have to live and work with the consequences of such decline.[71]

Attendance at a college or university after high school has become a "default decision"[72] that remains largely unquestioned by teachers, parents, or families. Equally held is the belief that if children work hard enough they will have equal access to this postsecondary education. This tenet is increasingly problematic as the gaps between the rich and poor and correspondingly gaps in the public education offered across different communities in this country become ever-wider, as equal opportunity in education becomes an ever-elusive myth.

Education as Equal Opportunity

For many, education is viewed as a means to provide equal opportunities for all.[73] Often these considerations fail to account not only for the nonstandard conditions outlined above, but also for social structures that have long discriminated based on race, class, gender, and other issues. Yet it seems that we must view the tenet that education can directly reduce inequalities with skepticism, particularly when we see the vast disparaties in educational conditions offered to children throughout the country. While some children lack books and basic services in their schools, others have state-of-the-art classrooms and technology available to them. The differences in school conditions only scratch the surface of the differences in community and home conditions. The ever-widening gap between the rich and poor in the United States has had significant consequences for the children and school students in this country.

The dominant belief that education would equalize the playing field for students from all backgrounds was part of the liberal ideology of many of Prairie Town's educators. One first grade teacher explained:

Our children out here are going to be competing, and I don't like the word competing, but they are going to be working with people from large settings, and our children need as good of an education as [other children] are getting.[74]

Within neoliberal contexts, this "equal education" was increasingly difficult to achieve:

In the emerging economy, success will depend most on talent, ingenuity, the ability to sell oneself, and connections. The quality of a child's early education and the character of a child's community are centrally important in these respects. Yet with ever-increasing efficiency, the sorting mechanism is separating children according to the communities and the schools their parents can best afford.[75]

For those who read Prairie Town through a neoliberal lens, there was little hope their children would have the necessary "connections" that would enable them to meet with at least this definition of economic success, particularly as they saw class sizes growing because teacher positions were being cut, and resources and programs dwindling. One parent stated:

I don't appreciate that they keep cutting [resources and programs in Prairie Town]. . . . I guess if I were job shopping, and I came here and saw this 85 year old building, would I want my children [here] or would I want to go to Alexandria where they have brand new buildings? If my children were going to be in the classroom with 30 or 35 students I would pull them . . . I don't think it's fair to the students to keep jamming them into tighter and tighter classrooms . . . but I'm a taxpayer too, and I don't always want to see my taxes go up, but you do what you have to do to get a quality school for your children.

She went on to share her frustration over proposed cuts to the music program:

[I]t's going to be a real struggle to keep students in the band program because they're switching that around and the person that they're asking to take over the band is not going to be well-received . . . and music is a core curriculum subject, it's not an extra-curricular. Then why aren't they given that opportunity? Why are we saying, "Well here, we'll just put this [unqualified] person in your classroom to teach you." They wouldn't do that in the other [subject areas]. They aren't going to put a math major in the social studies room. So why are they doing that, you know, in this area? And that's just one little part of the whole problem. But it's going to breed contempt and it's going to breed distrust. Kids are going to drop out. They're not going to want it. And thereby are we hurting their long-range education plans? Are these kids that could have gotten music scholarships? I don't know. You hope that your child will [excel] in something, and if music happens to be their thing, there's plenty of children that have gone to college because they're good in music.[76]

The commonly held viewpoint that children needed to attend college to attain success is more than evident in this parent's comments. At the same time, she had legitimate concerns about the consequences continued cuts to the budget and resources in Prairie Town would bring to the children, cuts that would likely extend beyond music and band programs.

School curriculum and organization in rural areas are social structures that have worked over time to order children and schools, curriculum and knowledge, and ultimately society in particular ways.[77] For the majority of Americans, schooling as it currently exists is an expected ritual—a salient part of the routine of American life. Problematizing these rituals is often difficult because individuals tend to read schooling and their own relative success or failure at it as a private issue, rather than a public concern. In other words, many believe that schooling is organized as it is because it is for the good of the students—those who will work hard enough and are smart enough will succeed and others will not because of their own personal flaws. However, as Nespor[78] noted, the construction of school knowledge is neither objectively defined nor is it scientifically validated. Instead it is:

[A] social construction growing out of historical and structural processes, political conflicts, and human decisions. The outcomes of these processes, conflicts, and decisions . . . represent assertions about the nature of knowledge in the world.[79]

For Prairie Town, this means that rural education reflects particular knowledges that convey information to students about what is best and most valuable in this society. Because the education that is most valued is one that will lead to academic success, it reflects aspirations for class mobility, sending children a message that schooling will result in economic success and cultural prestige.

Implicit in this dominant Discourse are messages that life and goals that are different from the small rural community are more desirable, and those who stay behind to live in the rural community are somehow less successful. Schooling and academic competence emphasize particular kinds of capital, or social power relations, while rejecting others. In rural Prairie Town, as in many rural schools throughout the nation, the cultural capital valued most by the school was influenced by hegemonic societal trends toward capitalism, modernization, and middle class suburban norms, as it sent implicit, and sometimes explicit, messages that rural life was not of much value. Because neoliberalism was a dominant ideology, one that was relatively unquestioned, its primary values were passed relatively easily into the schools. As educator Colin Lankshear explained:

> [D]iscourses of dominant groups become those which dominate education, and become established as major legitimate routes to securing social goods (like wealth and status). As a result, educational success is patterned along distinct lines of prior discursive experience associated with membership of particular social groups.[80]

Parents and educators in Prairie Town, like parents and educators elsewhere, had high hopes that education will provide social mobility for their children. Because of this, there is no critique of the assumptions embedded in the Discourses dominating education. Rather, community members strategized in the town meetings, and probably other places, to ensure that the status quo could continue to be met or exceeded. The promotion of academic competence in particular regimes of knowledge that narrows the curriculum based on assumptions about student needs for postsecondary schooling and, of late, the accompanying expressed need to prepare workers for the neoliberal global economy, reflects the dominant educational ideology in many communities. Dominant structures and values, along with their embedded biases, emerge from complex processes by which those ideals of the dominant group come to be seen as natural and self-evident. In other words, subscription to the beliefs of the dominant discourse group is not always a conscious or knowing process, nor is it a conspiracy, and many in Prairie Town subscribe to this ideology because it seems reasonable and as such, remains largely unquestioned. It has long been accepted that schools play a role in determining student opportunities as they regulate access to particular Discourses, and Prairie Town's school is no exception to this.

However, this dominant ideology of school literacy does not necessarily serve all in the town or community well, and even in the brief look at the school offered in this chapter we see how the hegemonic Discourse results in exclusions or marginalizations of knowledges, literacies, and consequently children. Because of this, care must be taken to critically disrupt and question those taken-for-granted values and practices that serve some but not all of the members of a given community. This is important, partly due to Brian Street's concerns:

> [R]einforcement of schooled literacy in the community contributes, alongside that of the school itself, to the construction of identity and personhood in the modern nation-state.[81]

In other words, the ways in which education is read in communities have significant bearing on understandings that students and community members have about themselves—how they read themselves, their positions, and their subsequent responsibilities in the world. Different readings of the purposes of schools are possible, particularly if communities will engage a language of critique to question the status quo and norms that typically remain unquestioned. We'll now turn to this possibility, considering the way literacy is essential to it, as we conclude this chapter.

Having It Their Way

Neoliberalism as an ideology encouraged a reading of farms, communities, and education through capitalist principles that sought to commodify all aspects of American life, equating citizenship with consumerism and fostering a belief that business and industry principles were ideal. In other words, the signs, symbols, and texts of various aspects of rural life were read in the same ways the signs, symbols, and texts of businesses were read.[82] As such, attention was directed toward expanding while at the same time increasingly centralizing production in the hands of a few, increasing efficiency of operations, and creating markets where profits could be realized.

Through neoliberalism and farmers' work to increase production, farms essentially became "factories in the field."[83] For those farmers who began to read their farms as factories, there was the ever-present need to expand, to produce more per acre, and to sell more. These farmers attended to the capitalist texts, including larger and more efficient technologies, frequently at the expense of human suffering. In other words, some compromised their own well-being and their neighbors' as they put aside agrarian ideals and human and environmental concerns in order to survive financially in a brutal and wildly unpredictable marketplace.

Communities, like farms, were goods that could be bought or discarded, constituted by individuals who had no common plight other than their economic worth. When communities are read through neoliberal ideologies, the signs readers attend to include the prestige, material value, and cultural capital that a community will bring. Those who live in communities that do not necessarily have economic or cultural power, like Prairie Town, and look for neoliberal values find themselves frustrated by their surroundings as they see only shortcomings in the community. These readers can not recognize symbols that run below the surface of their own materiality that may indicate value or worth in a rural lifestyle. Similarly, they do not necessarily grasp the hidden forces that may ultimately contribute to their demise as they become increasingly separated from others in the competitive effort to have more, produce more, and make more. Typically, the only hope they see for the future is to increase the cultural and economic power of their community through "renewal" projects that make them appealing to investors and corporations, projects that will eventually consume the community and contribute to its end. As the drive for free trade compromised basic human freedoms, particularly those Marshall Berman describes as affirming oneself and also recognizing that others are free as well, those who read the world with neoliberal notions in mind failed to notice the consequences so-called free trade would bring, even to their own community.

In the same way communities became goods, schools became commodified spaces where, according to neoliberal logic, the principles of business could be applied to the school system in order to increase output among human capital.[84] Schools were increasingly cast as symbols of capitalist production where knowledge could be commodified and children could be sorted based on their potential value to contribute to the cultural and economic capital of U.S. dominance.[85] School reforms that enhanced efficiency, standardized the means of production, and measured outputs and production increases were deemed reasonable reforms. Yet, as we saw in this chapter, efforts to standardize and homogenize output occurred in places where conditions and resources were not standard. Further, as such efforts worked to marginalize differences, many children were left out of the education success equation. The social and human consequences of this omission are becoming a difficult reality in many communities throughout the nation, including rural communities that have high dropout rates, particularly among minority and immigrant students whose parents are workers in local meat packing plants.

Just as Burger King perpetuated an illusion of choice in rural Prairie Town, neoliberal ideologies likewise forwarded a view that alternatives are possible and available to any individual who will so choose. Neoliberals often frame the possibilities of choice as "personal choice,"[86] further privatizing the issues many individuals, communities, and schools face, removing the potential for discussion and critical engagement of social issues into a private realm. At the same time, it seems increasingly difficult to engage discussions that disrupt commonly held beliefs about what it means to live and work in the United States. Neoliberalism's hegemony has infiltrated the consciousness of American citizens to such a large degree that employing any language of critique, suggesting different ways to read the circumstances in which we live, is difficult to do. Yet if we can step away from our present conditions and "try on" a different ideology, even temporarily, we may begin to read the world a little differently and in turn to imagine different possibilities. Part of this "stepping away" necessarily involves a critique of our present circumstances. As Pierre Bourdieu suggested, "to master the future one needs a hold on the present."[87] Likewise the critique of the present and efforts to move toward a new and better future require new languages and literacies. These possibilities are the subject of the next two chapters as we consider hope for the future in Prairie Town and the possibilities for radical change in rural communities.

Part III

Toward a New Rural Literacy

Chapter 5
A Prairie Renaissance

The conception of politics that we defend is far from the idea that "everything is possible." In fact, it's an immense task to try to propose a few possibles, in the plural—a few possibilities other than what we are told is possible. It is a matter of showing how the space of the possible is larger than the one we are assigned—that something else is possible, but not that everything is possible.[1]

When we were in Prairie Town, we lived close to a small park where the boys played basketball, rode their bicycles, and spun seemingly endlessly on a merry-go-round that reflected light streaming through the leaves of the tall ash trees surrounding the park's perimeter. Our afternoons were frequently spent enjoying the quiet calm the park afforded, and we sometimes selfishly thought of the park as our own. Rarely was anyone else visiting when we were there.

One day as we walked to the park, we noticed that a house had been placed on an empty lot just down the street from our home. It was a simple two-story structure, and the house itself, weatherworn and plain as it was with windows that seemed too small for its large front, was not particularly remarkable. We decided it must have been special to someone—they went to a lot of trouble to move the old house in to town. Over the next months, we watched as the house was carefully transformed with new siding, shiny brass light fixtures, a new garage on the side, and a new front porch. We were curious about what would become of it, often wagering guesses as we ate our dinner, until one day our bets came to an end when a "For Sale" sign was perfunctorily posted in the front yard. The new old house, which seemed to be lovingly remodeled, remained on the market for several months, and when we drove away from Prairie Town, it remained vacant.

The house perplexed us in many ways. Living as we do in a society that consumes more than it preserves, we couldn't figure out why someone would go to so much trouble over an old and seemingly unremarkable house. With the remodeling efforts clearly visible from our dining room window, we often discussed whether it would be easier, and perhaps less costly, to just build a new energy efficient house and leave the old house to its fate elsewhere. At the same time, we found it interesting that someone cared enough to restore it, and knowing what we did about the rural community where we lived, we were not particularly surprised. We had met enough people who shared a commitment to "restoration," at least in the community sense. While society often devalued rural life and experiences, willing to discard them for shiny new, convenient communities efficiently built elsewhere, some in Prairie Town were not deterred. Community participation and renewal efforts seemed to be an expected integral part of the Discourse of rural life for many of our neighbors and friends. In fact, Prairie Renaissance, a particularly ambitious community organizing effort detailed later in this chapter, was just under way around the time the house was moved to our street. Like the old house, people in town were committed to restoring their community, and they worked to gain control over the meanings and literacies this effort entailed. This chapter shares these efforts, using examples of community participation and planning in public spaces that were evident in school board and town meetings, two of the most common venues for public participation in Prairie Town. These examples of public engagement and democratic participation demonstrate the ways in which some in the community have worked to control the meanings of rural life and the ways in which they hope to live and work in a globalized society. In these public spaces, we find examples of the ways in which various literacies surface as individuals draw on sometimes competing ideologies to read their world and its possibilities. To begin, we'll consider a recent school board meeting where different literacies were evident. This section offers a brief review of the traditional literacy and neoliberal literacy before moving on to the main purpose of the chapter: to explain the characteristics of the new agrarian literacy that is developing in Prairie Town.

Traditional Literacies

Just as the old house was carefully preserved down the street from our own home, there were efforts in Prairie Town to preserve other aspects of rural life. Typically these efforts were most evident in public gatherings in Prairie Town where discussions about how to preserve traditional rural life occurred. The public gatherings most often took form as town and school board meetings, venues that were well attended, particularly if a controversial topic was at hand. Listening carefully at these meetings as individuals discussed the purposes of education and visions for rural life provided insight into the literacies various individuals and groups employed as they attempted to negotiate their lives together in rural Prairie Town.

One recent meeting offers a particularly poignant example of the various literacies that circulate in and among these public forums. During the April 17, 2002 school board meeting, a parent addressed the school board, expressing his concern that people were brought in to the school to speak to the boys' eighth grade health class and the eleventh and twelfth grade foods classes about vegetarianism and vegan diets. The parent explained that the speakers, whom he felt would not have met the school's dress code, focused more on animal rights issues than nutritional information. The parent seemed particularly troubled that such a presentation was disrespectful of the local students and families who worked in animal agriculture. He explained to the board, "We have some of the best livestock producers in the state and country [in Prairie Town]."[2] Two school board members, one who was a former teacher, echoed the parent's concerns by stating that "counter culture" speakers should not be allowed to address students in the school and that the past three years have resulted in things "creeping into the school" that should not be permitted.[3] Another parent continued the conversation by suggesting that the school had "lost its purpose in the last two or three years and [had] gotten away from teaching the basics. Instead, he said, it's trying to address social issues."[4] One school board member disagreed, stating that the purpose of the local school was to prepare students for the "big world" where they would inevitably find controversy.[5] Meanwhile, others in attendance deliberated whether such controversy would lead to parents open-enrolling their children to another school, an action that would further contribute to the loss of economic revenues in the district. (This last point will be taken up in the next section of this chapter.)

This brief exchange reflects tensions and ideological struggles that exist in the community as diverse ideologies drive particular readings of rural life and education and the possibilities both afford. In this account, there are texts that are read differently by different individuals. The concerned parent read pride in local animal agriculture. Agrarian ideologies influenced this reading in a way that was evidenced in his hope to protect this local industry, as opposed to introducing changes in local agriculture that would be more aligned with the vegetarians' talk (for example, organic and other vegetarian and/or sustainable farming methods). In addition, this parent read the purposes and functions of schooling through a more traditional lens, hoping it would preserve the local status quo, thus protecting local interests and livelihoods without introducing potential controversy. This reading was influenced by a conservative ideology that is often aligned with nostalgia for and (mis)perceptions of a more homogeneous past (hence, conservative calls for "back to basics" movements in education). This reading worked to politicize schools by indoctrinating individuals to believe there is only one set of values that should direct schooling in the United States. Similarly, the school board members who concurred with the concerned parent likewise read schooling through a conservative ideological position that expected education to remain "neutral" and "uncontroversial," and likewise expects that educators should refrain from presenting alternative visions or possibilities to students. Such a conservative ideology anticipates that schools should protect children from any possible aberration (or counterculture) and avoid potential controversy.

In addition to this traditional literacy, there were alternative literacies evident in the discussion of vegetarianism at the school board meeting. In fact, there have always been alternative literacies in Prairie Town, as we saw in chapter 3, some of which are recognized and valued more readily than others are. In what follows, we'll discuss two of the alternative literacies that surfaced at the school board meeting—neoliberal literacy and a new agrarian literacy.

Neoliberal Literacies

For some reason, the "for sale" sign in the front of the restored home really bothered me. I couldn't seem to understand how someone could put so much care into a project, and then put a price tag on it. Unfortunately, I didn't have the opportunity to ask those restoring the home about this. As soon as the sign was posted in the yard, no one seemed to return to check on the place, and the house fell strangely silent after months of busy activity. At the same time, however, I suppose I shouldn't have been surprised. It seemed like everything was fair game for the market. There was talk among different constituencies in the community about marketing the town for tourists (even though there wasn't a recreational lake in the county) and discussions about whether rural ways of life could be bought and sold. A Minnesota Tourist group proposed to advertise for Prairie Town, at a price of $7,500 per year, and even though the city council rejected the proposal, the notion of marketing rural life was still in the air. Living as we were in the context of neoliberal influences, it seemed that profit was always a priority and that everything could be subjected to the laws of the market. This extension of capitalist principles to the selling of rural ways of life reflected a pervasive and largely unquestioned belief that capitalism could solve social issues.

Similarly, the school board meeting exchange about the controversy over the vegetarian presentation demonstrates the ideological hold neoliberalism had on some readings of events in the community. Rather than engage in a discussion about curriculum, children, or families, what was foremost on some of the school board members' and audience's minds was the fact that any measure of controversy about the school could lead some to enroll their children elsewhere, thus driving down an already dwindling budget.[6] Open enrollment policies in Minnesota were designed so that parents have "choice" to enroll their children in any public school, whether it is in their home district or not. This policy, in accordance with neoliberal principles, endorsed competition among schools. As such, schools would need to compete with their neighbors to keep enrollment, and consequently revenue, high. If a school was not perceived to be performing well, parents could take their children elsewhere. In this way, as schools are subject to the "free market," poor strategizing by individuals (rather than publics committed to supporting public education), which in this case involved introducing a potentially controversial topic in school, would lead to a failed social project (i.e., public education).

The one school board member who seemed to object to the claim that the vegetarians had no place in the school argued that Prairie Town's children needed to be prepared to go out into the world, where they would inevitably find controversy. He too employed a neoliberal literacy, albeit with a different argument, by implicitly suggesting that the school needed to prepare students to go into the world with a high degree of human capital, part of which involved the ability to negotiate controversy. Because neoliberalism was a dominant ideology, the appropriateness of considering children as human capital or the propriety of endorsing free market values in public education was rarely questioned when decisions about schooling were made. For example, few, if any, seemed concerned about the consequences open enrollment might have, particularly as the policy worked in surveillance of curriculum, teachers, and administrators. In other words, the open enrollment policy, imbued as it was with capitalist notions that competition would result in higher performance in schools, had a normalizing effect that worked to keep curriculum and teachers within particular, seemingly "safe" and uncontroversial parameters.[7] Increasingly these "safe" parameters endorsed a functionalist plan for schooling that espoused job training as the ideal curriculum for schools. Those who read schools through a neoliberal ideological lens were uncomfortable with any diversion from these prescribed tasks or any controversy that might jeopardize the ability of schools to lead students successfully into the job market. In this case, if Prairie Town's school funding was compromised, it would affect the school's survival. "Better safe than sorry" seemed an appropriate slogan for those who would want the school to receive adequate funding rather than broach alternative discourses with students.

Because the neoliberal reading of the vegetarian presentation rejected the content of the talk, just as the more traditional reading did, it appeared that there was consensus at the meeting that such topics were unacceptable. Yet, the basis for the rejection was quite different. The more traditional reading expected that schools should teach seemingly apolitical skills and should not consider social issues or controversial topics. The neoliberal reading found the vegetarian presentation to jeopardize the ability for Prairie Town's school to compete for students. Both positions found unsatisfactory meaning in the presentation which resulted in rejection of the event. These different perspectives were in conflict with a third position, one that did not receive much attention either at the meeting or in the newspaper account—that of the vegetarians. In what follows, we'll consider this third literacy, one that reads the availability of choice in the community. This third literacy at the school board meeting, a new agrarian literacy, will then be connected to a broader public forum in Prairie Town, the Prairie Renaissance project.

A New Agrarian Literacy

While the newspaper account and school board members paid little attention to it, the vegetarians who conducted the presentation at the high school, along with the teacher who arranged for the talk, offered the students an alternative literacy, a way of reading the world in rural Prairie Town that was different from what the traditional or neoliberal literacies endorsed. The vegetarians suggested that the students did not have to leave the community in order to have choices about how they would live in Prairie Town. Instead, they proposed that the students could have control over decisions that affected their lives. Although this occurred within a different context, their presentation was not unlike that of the economic advisor, who suggested that choices were available in Prairie Town and that young people could live well without leaving the community. It was not the content of their talk that necessarily contributed to the new agrarian literacy; instead it was the purpose—the proposal that choices could be made even if you lived in the town. While meat-based diets were part of the mainstream in the community (there was even a "Beef Month" each spring), the vegetarians pointed out that there were choices about diet and different viewpoints with respect to the animal livestock that was part of agriculture in the region. Different meanings could be read in food production and consumption. Meat-based diets could be read as a less healthy option in comparison to vegetarian diets, while animal production and slaughterhouse practices could represent a wastefulness of water and land when compared to vegetarian and organic farming practices. While there was no mention of it at the school board meeting, some in Prairie Town had already organized to provide different food alternatives through the community's food cooperative. The cooperative, managed and operated by local volunteers, offered organic and vegetarian foods to the community, and it was largely driven by the choices people in Prairie Town wanted to have. Suggestions for food options could be made to the cooperative, and the alternative foods could be ordered. While it was not a particularly large operation, situated in approximately 300 square feet of space behind a store on Main Street, it was the one place in town where organic and vegetarian food products could be purchased.

The vegetarians' suggestion that young people could live differently while they resided in Prairie Town came at a time when many young people and adults were working together through a series of public meetings to control the meanings and conditions of rural life. This effort, the Prairie Renaissance project, included a series of public town meetings where individuals worked together to define what the community meant, a definition that spanned its past, present, and future. In the remainder of this chapter, we'll first consider a general description of these town meetings, followed by an extended discussion of their contribution to the new agrarian literacy in Prairie Town, one that valued open dialogue, control individuals had over their own lives, and the possibility for choices.

Prairie Renaissance: A Description of the Project

The word "renaissance" typically indicates a rebirth or new beginning. Historically, we tend to think of the Renaissance as a time of change in European arts, economics, and science that occurred between 1300 and 1650. Gutenberg's printing press and thinkers and artists from Martin Luther and John Calvin to Galileo and Michelangelo changed the way people understood the world. Their original thinking seems to be central to any understanding of "renaissance." It was in this spirit, and with a hope for original thinking, that Prairie Town's effort to forge a new beginning was founded. The Prairie Renaissance reflects a new agrarian literacy, a way of reading local life that draws on the past, is aware of the market, but simultaneously works for human participation in decisions about the local community.

Prairie Town's "Prairie Renaissance" project was formalized when a group of residents who participated in a local leadership program joined a Blandin Community Leadership Program (BCLP) in order to achieve a more intensive focus on individual and community leadership skills.[8] The Blandin Foundation, a Minnesota-based philanthropy, began its rural community leadership program in 1985. The leadership program was organized around the concept of building and maintaining healthy communities, which they described as "a place to live where all people can meet their economic, social, physical and cultural needs, work together for the common good, and participate in creating their future."[9] With attention to multifaceted aspects of rural communities, the foundation encourages individuals to identify both strengths and weaknesses of the community in an effort to find solutions and strategies that would in turn benefit the community.

As the Prairie Town leadership group was beginning its work in the fall of 1998, alumni[10] of the same program throughout the state of Minnesota asked the Blandin Foundation for a "next step," for community projects to work on in the state so they might practice what they learned. As a result, Blandin established a second program, the Blandin Community Investment Partnership (BCIP), piloted in December 1998. As the BCLP group finished in Prairie Town, the Center for Small Towns at the nearby university campus applied for a grant from Blandin to participate in the BCIP. Blandin suggested that the Center for Small Towns facilitate planning for communities throughout western Minnesota, beginning with Prairie Town. The preliminary town meeting, held in January 1999, began the process of generating local interest and participation in the program. This meeting brought university and local people together to forge a vision for how they might live together. This was an important effort because, while the university had been part of the community since the 1960s, there often remained a large gap between the town and university people. Prairie Town's mayor explained:

> Let's face it. Thirty, forty years ago, the number of college educated people [was] smaller than it is today. And there were those that thought that we certainly didn't need to bring those kind of people in here. They were too smart.

They knew things. And they had different ideas than our rural setting does. It was kind of threatening and scary at the same time. And I thought that possibly, we've had one generation actually now, that that would have disappeared.[11]

Prairie Town's economic advisor likewise expressed concern about the apparent division between the university and the community when he stated:

> There are people up at the university that have been teaching there for 20 years and I've never seen them in town. . . . But there's also a townie attitude toward the university, especially among the older population. "Them dope-smoking eggheads," you know. But I think that . . . it's changing . . . it's not as tough as it was.[12]

The Prairie Renaissance brought 142 people that spanned five age cohorts (under twenty-one years of age to over seventy years of age) from the university and town together in a collective project, trying to establish a commitment to place and a sense of community that spanned diverse ideologies and literacies. The town meeting format permitted the expression of a range of views and opinions and a collective understanding of others' hopes for the community. This involved a sophisticated negotiation of various groups in the community in order to read both what was said and unsaid during the meetings. As one teacher of Norwegian heritage politely reminded me during a public meeting, some of the people in Prairie Town would just keep things to themselves rather than speak out in public. She explained that it was "just the way Norwegians were." For those who led these town meetings, there had to be alternative ways for people to voice their opinions and concerns other than speaking in a public session. Opinions could be privately expressed through phone calls to meeting facilitators, email or Internet correspondence, or in writing. Likewise, facilitators of town meetings had to be able to read the gestures and expressions of those in attendance. If someone seemed dissatisfied but did not express their dissatisfaction, the facilitators would need to speak with them in a private forum.

During the first set of town meetings, those participating developed a vision statement to guide their work. The vision statement articulated goals in areas of economic opportunity, recreation/culture, community leadership, infrastructure/services, lifelong learning, and valuing diversity. The subtheme of the meetings, as articulated in a narrative written by the project coordinator, included:

> [C]onnecting our community, first to itself, and then to the world. The designated projects all foster a connection of people to people, people to resources, and our community to the surrounding communities. Having successfully constructed a strong infrastructure of service, support, and accessibility the community is equipped to reach beyond its borders and impact a wider world.[13]

A local high school student designed the logo that appeared on the letterhead and other correspondence regarding the Prairie Renaissance project. It stated: "Pulling it Together: Our greatest resource is people." The logo implicitly suggested that the community had not been together and that solidarity and a focus on the people in Prairie Town should be foremost in any plan for the future. Included in the logo are the words diversity, leadership, improvement, and cooperation, with corresponding images of a globe, a small community, a person standing behind a lectern, and two joined hands with different skin colors. The combination of these words and images represents the group's larger vision for its community, some that may be attainable and others not, but largely it was a project of possibility, an effort to simultaneously determine what they might do in relation to their broader cultural, political, and social projects.[14] Ideologically, members of this group began to reinsert values of collective responsibility that were part of the democratic socialist and populist ideologies of earlier communities throughout the region. They looked at their community—the people and its objects—and read hope in the possibilities they might attain together. While there may have been some dissent around the particulars, there was a broad consensus in values as they worked to gain control over local meanings. In light of this, they identified three somewhat overlapping "priority" areas to begin their work: (1) economic/environment, (2) recreation/culture, and (3) young people. General goals were written to improve these priority areas, followed by more specific projects in relation to these statements.

While the Prairie Town Renaissance group's broader cultural and political projects engaged questions about how they might live together into the future, there was a shared sense of urgency to engage in action that would stave off emigration from rural areas to urban and suburban centers. There was a similar commitment to change accompanying perceptions that rural areas do not offer comparable cultural and economic opportunities. As such, the group articulated a plan to "change contemporary thinking regarding rural or non-metro life by initiating . . . a revival of interest in and access to the valuable assets that are available . . . on the prairie."[15] Consequently, the group identified short-term, attainable goals that would make living in Prairie Town more appealing to young and old alike. These goals drew on the past, but had an eye toward the market and the ways in which they might control market forces in Prairie Town.

As an example, one of the goals identified by the group included establishing a local business exposition that would improve the economic environment in the area. The exposition would showcase local businesses and help to give Prairie Town's youth experience with local employment opportunities. This goal corresponded with the Prairie Renaissance group's articulated goal of keeping money within the community and encouraging young people to stay in Prairie Town. The vision statement for Prairie Renaissance specifically mentioned the hope that Prairie Town would be an economically stable community with locally owned and community-based businesses.[16] By July 2000, just a little over a year after the first Prairie Renaissance meeting, the First Annual Prairie Industrial/Business Expo was held during a local community fair. The exposition showcased twelve local businesses and was reported to have favorable reviews.

The Prairie Renaissance group was also interested in local culture and the arts. In light of this, the Minnesota Rural Arts Initiative was contracted to recruit local and regional artists, historians, and storytellers to "dig into the heart and soul of [Prairie Town]."[17] In an effort to better understand the local culture and how it is expressed, a group of storytellers shared memories with interested community members, conveying their knowledge about where the community was, where it is today, and where it might go in the future. This activity was part of a broader "culture incubator" project that would develop theater, the arts, and music in the community. These cultural activities would work to link the community to itself, and it would also help to "keep entertainment dollars in the community."[18] In this effort, we see attempts to value the local culture and to connect the present and future to the past.

A third priority included providing local youth with opportunities and recreational activities. One project in relation to this priority was building a youth recreation/skate park. Prairie Town's young people led this effort by researching and proposing the project to the town and local government officials. This endeavor included collecting information on regulations, costs, matching contributions, and locations. This was no small undertaking, and after two years of time and effort, more than thirty high school students and twenty to twenty-five adults developed the Skate Park to the point where a contractor was identified, and a fundraising campaign was under way. Through this project, young people in the community learned that they could change their current conditions, and that it wasn't necessary to leave town to do so. In spite of voiced opposition by some in the community that a skate park was "not safe" and just "not a good idea," the young people were able to move ahead with their plans. In August 2001, the skate park opened, and a formal grand opening was scheduled for July 2002, complete with demonstrations and games. More than $40,000 was raised for the park, and young people from throughout the region drove in carloads to Prairie Town to enjoy it.

Through the Renaissance project, a new agrarian literacy was emerging in Prairie Town. This new literacy was connected to the past, but it attempted to disrupt some of the more problematic aspects of a traditional literacy, particularly the racism and resistance to cultural diversity that is often inherent in more traditional literacies. At the same time, this new literacy read hope, rather than despair, in the current rural condition as it recognized the potential that collective solidarity might bring. The Prairie Renaissance group recognized the importance of interdependence across the community as a first step toward connecting their community to other communities. As a group, they were working against neoliberal literacies, ways of reading the world that were influenced by ideologies that valued privatization and competition. As David Sehr explained:

> The privatized and individualistic ideologies that currently dominate people's understandings of the world deny and disguise the reality of people's interdependence. These ideologies encourage individuals intentionally to close their eyes to the social consequences of their actions or their inaction. They replace conscious individual responsibility for shaping society, with blind faith in an economistic invisible hand. This produces the oft-repeated sentiment that market forces will solve all of society's problems. These privatistic ideologies deny that people can consciously shape their own social future. They deny in principle that people can rule themselves.[19]

Rather than closing their eyes, the Prairie Renaissance group was helping others in the community to develop choices and to read the texts of their rural community in different ways. Rather than reading the community as a place where there was "nothing to do," the Renaissance group helped the young people in particular to read possibilities and to develop literacies that would allow them to shape the community in ways they wanted, whether through work, recreation, or the arts. This literacy, which continues to evolve as the Renaissance group engages in this ongoing work, always drew on the past as it continually connected and reconnected the histories of the town to the present and considered the conditions of the present to inform the future. Together the group continues to work toward a vision of the future that would reshape the town in ways they control.

Paul Theobald[20] noted that the restoration of community in rural areas must begin with a different set of assumptions than those that guided the early settlements. The work of community restoration, much like the work on the old house near where we lived, is different from building a brand new community where one didn't exist before. There are some aspects that need to be carefully preserved and other aspects that need to be discarded. There are foundations and frameworks that need to be kept in place and others that may be in need of much repair. It is a deliberate, tedious, and sometimes a painfully slow process, but it seems that, at least in Prairie Town, it was worth the effort. Given what I have come to know about this community, I expect this effort will continue in ways that will enrich people's lives in Prairie Town, and I doubt that it will culminate in a "for sale" sign being placed on the community.

In Prairie Town, the Renaissance group and public meetings offer opportunities for us to consider what a new agrarian literacy might be in more general contexts. Three characteristics of this new agrarian literacy seem particularly salient, and worth discussing in more detail: the open narrative, the effort to gain control of lives, and the opportunity for choices. As we consider these three characteristics, my hope is that other rural communities may find ways to connect to and learn from the efforts in Prairie Town.

Open Narratives

Public participation in Prairie Town is part of the culture of the community, an accepted and expected activity for those who live there. In part, this participation is driven by dissatisfaction with the current rural condition and a hope to bring about change in the community. As Zygmunt Bauman reminded us:

> [H]istorical change happens because humans are mortified and annoyed by what they find painful and unpalatable in their condition, because they do not wish these conditions to persist, and because they seek the way to mollify or redress their suffering.[21]

In some ways, Prairie Town has worked foremost against having its citizens' space and lives colonized by corporate culture. They've decided to reject large corporations in favor of local businesses, and they've recently made efforts to educate their young people about the possibilities they may find if they stay in the community. They've acknowledged, at least at some level, that cultural diversity is something they need to embrace, and they've begun public meetings to address this matter. Through collective efforts, they have taken on the difficult challenge of working against the individualism that is so often typical of American communities:

> A byproduct of our liberal democracy, as Alexis de Tocqueville noted, is an individualism that inclines us to look after ourselves and our increasingly small and scattered nuclear families rather than our neighbors, our communities, our nation. Participation in local government and civic associations used to combat this cultural tendency, and yet, especially during the last few decades, it would seem that individualism has won. This is not surprising since our emphasis on individual rights leads us to carve out our own personal spheres and gives us the justification for doing so. Once such rugged individualism takes hold, it makes collective action difficult at best. Participatory democracy, however, requires that some individuals overcome these inclinations by getting involved in local government, in mutual assistance, in Putnam's bowling leagues, and in civic associations of all kinds—the essential elements of democratic society.[22]

Through their acts of public participation and engagement, we see a commitment to participatory democracy through open narrative that enables Prairie Town's residents to voice not only their discontent with the current rural conditions they face, but also to work toward a future that is controlled by them. In their deliberations, we find evidence of the multiple literacies that have a place in Prairie Town, and within a democratic society these literacies, these ways of reading the world, have a right to be recognized.

No concept of citizenship and public space is neutral, and the ways in which public spaces and other venues for participatory practices are organized will always involve someone or some group's vision of who will participate and what the end product might be. In Prairie Town, these spaces were designed for open narrative and driven by a belief that participation and people's ideas were important. Recognition of the literacies and the inherent contradictions of the ideologies that direct the organization of public space and the content of public talk, along with the power relations that either confine or enable them, provide an opportunity for public pedagogy, for teaching about the possibilities and alternatives each literacy affords. In other words, each literacy is never equally recognized, and some are effectively silenced (as we noted in the press and the public's limited attention to the literacy the vegetarians and school teacher employed). Further, each literacy is not equally able to offer viable solutions to sustain the community. Neoliberal literacy, as one example, constrains the purposes of schooling in ways that conform to the status quo, and it similarly works to destroy small and rural schools as competition and inadequate funding models bring sometimes insurmountable economic challenges. Meanwhile, neoliberal literacy frequently works to the demise of the community as it leads the young people away from rural areas—"all that's solid melts into air."[23] As another example, we can see how traditional literacies hope for a past that is often steeped in myths, and is unattainable.

The broader purpose of public pedagogy should be to link the local meanings and practices in Prairie Town to similar meanings, practices, and struggles in other parts of the country and the world in what Imre Szeman describes as a globalization pedagogy.[24] Central to such a pedagogy should be a consideration of these literacies, or what Brian Street describes in a different context as the development of the awareness of the "socially and ideologically constructed nature of the specific forms we inhabit and use at given times."[25] In this way, by listening carefully to the open narrative in the public forums, we can consider how people and groups come to influence and draw on different literacies in relation to their various ideologies and visions for society. This consideration can then work toward the development of multiple literacies, multiple readings of the world, rather than the dominant tendency toward one-dimensional thought, or the inclination to conform to existing thought and behavior without any critical dimensions that might "transcend the existing society."[26] As Henry Giroux explained:

[A] critical public pedagogy should ascertain how certain meanings under particular historical conditions become more legitimate as representations of reality and take on the force of common sense assumptions shaping a broader set of discourses and social configurations at work in the dominant social order.[27]

In other words, those who share a commitment to rural life share particular contexts, and their perspectives are central to reshaping dominant understandings of what it means to live and work in rural areas. The possibilities for such a project, for making literacy central to a critical public pedagogy that would link Prairie Town's efforts first to the local and then to other groups in a way that considers shared meanings and possibilities, will link Prairie Town to broader political projects. Recognition of these multiple literacies in Prairie Town allows us to engage in a critique that works to make public the contradictions and consequences each of these literacies offers.

To summarize, open narratives and attention to the meanings of rural life, of the symbolic and material conditions that rural communities face and the ways in which they are read by local peoples, should be central to the discussions and debates in the public spaces of the community. There should always be attention to the power relations and silences in these spaces as well. The goal of these discussions should not be to develop some perfect consensus, but instead to provide opportunities for various positions, for multiple literacies to be recognized and understood as the public space is used for public pedagogy and the articulation of a broader sense of shared goals. These shared goals can in turn become the starting place whereby individuals take action and gain more control over their lives.

Control of Lives

In Prairie Town, the Prairie Renaissance group used public space and the shared vision they developed to articulate a plan for action. While there may have been dissent about the particulars of this plan (for example, not everyone agreed about the value of the skate park in spite of the fact that all agreed the youth in the community needed recreational activities), individuals had the opportunity to participate in different ways to contribute to the broader goals. Not everyone had to agree, and not everyone did. But in the end, they all worked to gain control over the meanings, purposes, and organization of rural life. Rather than allowing outside forces, whether it be the "invisible hand of the market," laissez-faire economic policy, federal farm policy, or corporate farm contracts, to dictate the direction their lives should take, these individuals decided to collectively organize to regain control of the shape, form, and substance of their rural life.

As Chantal Mouffe[28] has reminded us, modern democracy requires an understanding that individuals have the right to organize their lives and realize them as they wish (a basic tenet of pluralism and liberal democracy). Yet at the same time, we need to recognize the fact that a perfect consensus is never fully realizable and should not be a goal. In other words, there will always be dissent and compromise in any democratic project, and the work of any democratic project will always be struggled over as it inherently involves values and relations of power. There will always be individuals who read the world differently, and some literacies will be more readily recognized over others. In Prairie Town, we saw an example of this in the struggle over the meanings and purposes of schooling in this small rural community, and we similarly found attempts by individuals to gain some control over these meanings.

Differences in reading the world should be valued, not discouraged or despised. Our literacies are multiple and intersecting, ever evolving and thus reflective of human agency. In other words, the meanings we understand from our world are generative and changing, and as human agents we transform and remake the world as we negotiate our readings of it with others.[29] As we come to recognize various literacies, the ways in which individuals read meaning in the multiple texts and signs in their culture, we come to understand the complexities that these literacies reflect and the possibilities for transformation they afford.

Sometimes individuals find they have competing literacies, competing ways of making sense of their world, and they draw on them at various times in different situations. In fact, Prairie Town's school board member who suggested the vegetarian presentation might help to better prepare students for the "big world" was involved in the development of a new agrarian literacy through the Prairie Renaissance project and other efforts to help youth live well in the community. His comments at the school board meeting, which implicitly suggested that students will one day need to leave Prairie Town, seemed to contradict the new agrarian literacy he was helping to develop through the Prairie Renaissance project. Through Prairie Renaissance he was working to help students read value in their community, to have control over their lives and to live well in Prairie

Town, and to, in turn, have choices about how they will live in the community. The fact that the new agrarian literacy was not evident in his talk at the school board meeting points to the complexities in the ways in which we all come to read the world. In different contexts and at different times, we draw on different literacies. In this way, our readings of the world are complex and situated, and they are enabled or constrained by particular social functions and contexts that inevitably are influenced by various power relations. As we come together to recognize these complexities and shared meanings among and across our differences, we can begin to link our private understandings and our personal struggles to more public and shared meanings that can in turn move democratic projects forward as we design and transform the world we live in.

Choices

The complexities and differences in reading the world allow us to imagine different possibilities and choices. We often live in the context of what sociologist Charles Lemert[30] has called "dead structures," a dead or deadly weight upon individuals which may limit our imaginations about how our lives may be different. While structures may be temporary or changing, for the most part, societal structures are salient and order our lives in particular ways. For example, there are societal structures in place that determine when and how we will gain a formal education, what kind of work we will do, what we should do with the money we earn, and more. Often these structures reflect power relations across individuals as they work to oppress some groups and empower others. Yet they typically seem natural and self-evident, and sometimes we do not even recognize them as such. Some structures are more powerful than others (for example, the "market"), and some are protected through power relations (think of the Skull and Bones society at Yale). From Karl Marx we learned that "we cannot understand ourselves in the present until we confront what is absent."[31] At the same time, we must confront what is also invisible (although not necessarily absent); that is, we must confront the power, structures, and ideologies that make our current state appear to be the only possibility. Our literacies reflect our understandings of these structures and absences, and multiliteracies enable us to question them and imagine different possibilities.

Some individuals and groups have more literacies to draw on than others as they imagine possibilities for the future. This is an important point for any public or globalized pedagogy. If we begin with the assumption that human learning is always situated, social, and cultural and is always embedded in material contexts,[32] we can interrogate and learn from the meanings that are generated and the literacies that are formed in the various Discourse communities in which we live. In this way, we can engage multiple literacies, multiple ways of reading the world, in new ways and in new forms so that we might imagine the choices available in understanding both what is possible and what is not. As such, we can then work to change the structures that order our lives and gain control over the ways in which are lives are shaped. Nothing social is inevitable. It is all constructed and it all can be changed.

Going Home

As we drove away from Prairie Town, we couldn't help glancing yet again at the empty house down the street from our own now empty home. We had come to Prairie Town with many of the social structures and neoliberal ideologies of our time directing our own literacies, our own understandings of the meanings and representations of our world. We were "travelers" striving to some extent for Robert Reich's definition of "success"[33] as we moved across the country to make a better living. While we didn't immediately notice it, we initially read Prairie Town with an eye toward its shortcomings, noting how the amenities we were accustomed to were not present, and we often thought about what the community needed to have to make it more like where we came from. While we found the "mom and pop" stores on Main Street to be quaint, we often drove forty-five minutes to shop at the closest Target retail store so we could have what we were accustomed to at prices we thought were reasonable. Yet, over time, as we listened to and engaged in the community, including the school board and town meetings, we came to learn the shortcomings of our own literacies and the richness of those that surrounded us. We began to read and to understand what others saw as valuable in the community, meanings we would have never shared had we just passed through the community.

In part, our own new agrarian literacy made us think about Pennsylvania, our home state that was, until the recent census redefined rural, considered the most rural in the nation. We wondered about how the literacies in Prairie Town connected up with some of the rural and often economically struggling communities we left behind. Not every rural community is the same, and while we found hope in Prairie Town's efforts toward a new literacy and social transformation, we questioned whether we would find similar possibilities in the communities where some of our own family members still lived. We knew these communities often had longer histories of economic decline than Prairie Town faced, and we wondered if hope was unrecoverable. Because of this, and because of a new sense of commitment to place, we returned home to see what we could learn and do. As we returned, we employed our new literacies as we attended to the meanings and signs of rural life as we considered the efforts of rural Pennsylvanians to gain control, to engage in open dialogue, and to have choices in their own communities. The final chapter of this book offers a glimpse at these efforts, and the ways in which Prairie Town's new agrarian literacy shares meanings and possibilities with rural people in Pennsylvania as well as other communities throughout the nation and the world.

Chapter 6
Joining Hands: Connecting Prairie Town to the World, and the World to Prairie Town

My driving destinations are different these days. Rather than driving wide flat prairie roads, looking for water towers or other landmarks to help me find my way, I navigate narrow, winding country roads that snake through the mountains and farmlands in rural Pennsylvania. Lately, I find myself driving north to a small community that was once a prosperous and bustling railroad town, and now has more than fifty years of economic decline. As incredulous as it may seem, the town seems to have fallen silent and forgotten amid the poverty that spans generations of families who hear reports of American prosperity elsewhere. Many of the children in this community live in the mountains that loom over the town, and too often their only shelter is an old hunting camp with dirt floors and no running water. These children spend their days at the local elementary school using computers and modern technology as their teachers hope to educate them well enough so they can be successful some day (i.e., leave town). Meanwhile, their parents struggle to find employment that will pay enough to change their lived conditions without landing them in jail.[1]

As I listen to the people who live in this "Hill Town" talk about their lives, I find the literacies they employ are similar in form to those who live in Prairie Town. There are people who at some times wish the community had the characteristics of its glory days, and they despair about the fact that old buildings and industry are gone and things aren't what they used to be. At the same time, some employ literacies that expect capitalism and neoliberal ideologies will solve their individual woes. As I read their local newspaper, for example, I find the representations they attend to are similar to those in Prairie Town. Usually there is a feature story about a former high school student who is attending a far-away university and has a bright future that will lead him or her even further away to find gainful employment. The newspaper increasingly marginalizes or fails to report stories about Hill Town, instead featuring events from other neighboring communities. This mis-reporting, which really is a form of censorship, fails to cover the reality people in Hill Town face, instead reporting on the reality of other people's lives. This point isn't lost on the readers, and recently a series of editorial comments attested to some residents' discomfort with this. The implicit, and increasingly explicit message, is that life is better elsewhere, and there is nothing worth noting in this town. I don't agree with that message, and I find much of interest in the community. In fact, my drive to Hill Town usually is related to a meeting with school and town leaders, many of whom are forward-looking and want to change the conditions the children in particular face. Our conversations frequently begin with talk of the weather and local events, much like Prairie Town conversations began, and then we invariably turn to more serious discussions of literacy and how literacy for liberation might be central in their efforts toward change.

What I've learned through these conversations is that the *content* of the literacies in Hill Town may differ from the content of literacies in Prairie Town, yet the characteristics of the literacies of the oppressed are similar in that they share despair, poverty, and suffering. In other words, in a broader sense, it is a literacy of the oppressed. What is needed instead is a form of literacy that develops a language so that people can understand how capitalism and the misuse of power are largely responsible for the conditions many people across the world face and how they might instead unite through a literacy that liberates and changes their lived condition.

Many in Hill Town employ traditional literacies as they read the signs and texts of their town. This literacy, like the literacy in Prairie Town, looks at the empty railroad yard and draws on nostalgia that seems to wish for and recreate a past that may have never been. Hill Town has a different history and different lived conditions than Prairie Town—the once eight-track wide railroad is no longer there, and the empty stockyard buildings are falling down amid an overgrown field. Yet the *form* of the traditional literacies they employ are similar. They both employ this form of literacy that reads their world with nostalgia and hope for the past. Similar points could be made about more dominant literacies that read the symbols of the community against the values neoliberalism endorses—growing the economy at any cost, framing social issues through economic solutions, and expecting that shared values will bring success. While the content of neoliberal literacy may be different in Hill Town and Prairie Town (for example, Hill Town doesn't have to decide whether a meat-processing plant should be brought into the community or not—a meat-packing plant wouldn't see this town as an efficient site for processing meat), the emphasis is the same.

There are people in both communities who are discussing how the community can be marketed and sold, and in Hill Town there is talk about developing the tourist industry around hang-gliding and other outdoors activities like hunting and fishing. Similarly, those who are working to realize change in these towns seem to value characteristics of the new agrarian literacy. The emphasis on open narrative, the hope to seek control and have the freedom to develop their own options, and the potential to work with these options cross these communities in spite of the fact that the choices they develop may differ.

This point, that our literacies, while situated in our own lives and contexts, connect us to others in spite of differences in content or detail, is the central argument of this final chapter. In what follows, we'll consider this point in more detail by considering three contexts—the ways in which literacies connect rural communities to each other, the ways in which these literacies connect rural communities to the world, and the ways in which these literacies connect us all. To begin, we'll look for commonalities in Prairie Town's literacies in relation to some of its rural neighbors.

Literacies That Cross Rural Communities

In Prairie Town, we found the beginning of a new agrarian literacy that valued open narratives reflecting local people's opinions and worked to offer choices that generated from the community rather than were offered by others. We saw people employing this literacy as they worked to gain control over their lives. Largely these efforts were directed toward staving off emigration from the town and attempts to diversify the local economy in ways that were controlled by local groups and in concert with broader perceptions of local values. This literacy, reading the world for signs of opportunities for control and transformation are not limited to Prairie Town, a fact we noted when we returned to our home in Pennsylvania.

After we returned to Pennsylvania, we found there was a real stink in many communities throughout the state. Corporate hog farms, in their greed, had overtaken many areas, and people were concerned about air quality and water pollution, the decreased property value of their homes and land, and the general quality of life that was threatened by these farms. On April 16, 2002, more than 300 township governments across the state of Pennsylvania sent messages to local legislators that people needed to have more say in relation to corporate agribusinesses. According to attorney Thomas Alan Linzey of the Community Environmental Defense Fund, the overwhelming message from people throughout the state was "Don't tread on local democracy!"[2] While these local townships were organizing against the corporate hog farms, the Pennsylvania Senate passed Bill 1413, in spite of the fact that the Pennsylvania State Association of Township Supervisors overwhelmingly opposed the legislation. Senate Bill 1413 prohibited local governments from adopting ordinances that restricted agricultural operations, in effect prohibiting townships from responding to citizens who hoped to protect their health, safety, and welfare.[3] This is how capitalism sacrifices the imperatives of democracy.

The controversies over corporate hog farms were shared in rural communities throughout the United States and other countries. In Springfield, Illinois, the attorney general's office sued HenCo Hogs, accused of allowing odors to unreasonably interfere with local residents' ability to enjoy their properties. Instead of paying a fine, the corporation was ordered to work with the University of Illinois to minimize the odor. It was also banned from expanding beyond 3,600 hogs without permission from local residents, and from spreading manure on New Year's Day, Easter, Mother's Day, Memorial Day, Father's Day, Independence Day, Labor Day, Thanksgiving, and Christmas.[4] Not too far from Springfield, in Martinsburg, Missouri, Cargill Pork Inc. illegally dumped hog waste into the Loutre, a Missouri River tributary, contaminating more than five miles of the river and killing 53,000 fish. The company, which has a 17,000-pig farm, was fined $1 million plus costs for violating the Clean Water Act and making false statements.[5] The responsibility for the corporate world, their lack of ethics and care for others,[6] carefully preserves neoliberal discourse while it continuously asks people to trust the private while demonizing the public. In Canada, Ontario and Alberta property owners near hog farms have organized to win property tax cuts, arguing that the farms harm their air, water, and land.[7] The Canadian hog population, estimated at 28.2 million, nearly outnumbers the Canadian human population of just over thirty million people.[8] There are similar efforts to make this a public issue in towns and countrysides throughout the United States and Canada.

Members of the different groups represented in these accounts have shared cultural understandings and shared literacies that organize, mediate, and regulate their social practices. The owners and operators of the corporations understand the need to increase size and efficiency in order to expand profits, and some feel such large-scale operations are essential to the safety, quality, and lower cost of food (neoliberal literacies). Others disagree, reading these corporate farming operations as symbols of the threat to small farmers, whom they believe are important to sustaining a particular local heritage (traditional literacy). Meanwhile, groups such as the Pennsylvanians for Responsible Agriculture and the 10,000 Friends of Pennsylvania encourage people to consider different options and models for sustainable local agriculture, including small scale farms, and to organize in ways that would give local groups control over their lives (new agrarian literacies).

These dominant symbols of rural life that cross an array of communities across the United States and the world have meanings that are read and shared with individuals and groups in Prairie Town and other rural towns. Increasingly the symbols that have come to dominate rural America have been corporate in nature—the large grain mills, the factory farms, and the meat processing plants. These symbols are read as necessary by some (neoliberal literacies) and as the demise of rural America by others (traditional and new agrarian literacies). In the absence of these corporate influences, the dominant symbols have often been empty Main Streets, empty railroad yards, and empty school grounds. These symbols are read as necessary by some (traditional literacies), as evidence that economic change is needed by others (neoliberal literacies), and with hope that life can be different by yet others (new agrarian literacies). Given the ongoing conditions in rural communities, it seems self-evident that there will be one or the other—empty Main Streets or corporate influences. However, as we saw in Prairie Town and other grassroots organizations, many individuals and groups are working to disrupt these images, to read old symbols differently, and to create new meanings for rural communities.

Considering the dominant symbols that have come to represent the rural place, as well as how these symbols have emerged, seems an appropriate starting place for the disruption of old meanings and a critique of dominant literacies. The dominant symbols, their representations, and the readings of them typically involve hegemonic processes that tend to pervade the everyday consciousness of those who live in and outside rural communities alike. In other words, it is important to consider how these symbols and the manner in which they are read legitimate the dominant society in ways that are not just or equitable for rural residents or other marginalized groups, including migrant farm workers. These issues are important, particularly as they influence public dispositions toward policies and actions that "seek to remedy, improve, or neglect a [community's] existing social, economic, and political conditions."[9] These public dispositions, both of rural and nonrural residents, need to be interrogated and changed in ways that bring about more just and equitable conditions for rural and nonrural residents alike. This can occur through concerted efforts to bring to the fore of people's consciousness the human suffering and loss that is a direct result of the ways in which many of these symbols are read and enacted. Efforts to change the consciousness of people, efforts toward a public and globalized pedagogy will place at its center teaching and learning about different literacies, about different ways of reading life and the human condition that considers both the conditions of "social and cultural learning and reproduction in the context of globalization *and* the way in which globalization itself constitutes a problem of and for pedagogy."[10] In Prairie Town's case, as in many rural communities, such pedagogy could include, among others, critically questioning neoliberal notions of "progressive change" that make rural depopulation trends seem "unfortunate but necessary."[11] By unveiling the inherent contradictions in neoliberal discourse, we open spaces to create a new literacy that opposes the notion that neoliberalism is the only viable discourse and simultaneously works to liberate. Such a literacy would take what we have learned from the violations imposed by Worldcom, Arthur Anderson, and other major corporations to disrupt the neoliberal status quo. Other issues that would inform the creation of this new literacy might include how popular (mis)understandings of the rural are drawn on to construct ideas about a rural status quo and the extent to which characterizations of rural match (or not) observations of demographic, social, and economic conditions. Increasingly, public pedagogy in rural communities includes learning about the potential for mobilizing against state and federal agendas that work to wrest control away from local peoples. Literacy is central to every aspect of this pedagogy, from reading and interpreting the signs, gestures, and representations of rural to mobilizing for change.

Questioning the dominant symbols of rural life and the ways in which they are read, considering the various literacies in the community, opens possibilities for an ideological critique. Such a critique in turn will allow the community and its members to imagine changes that extend to other people and contexts in ways that move beyond status quo solutions and prevailing rationalities. To begin, an ideological critique will allow some to see how certain ideologies, including socialist and agrarian tendencies, still circulate in the hearts and minds of those in the community in spite of the hegemonic influences of capitalism and neoliberalism. Opening this up for discussion allows for the engagement of a reflexive self-criticism that places resistance and human agency at the center of any effort to improve the human condition across multiple sites. In this way, we come to understand how humans appropriate, select, and generate meaning (i.e., what their literacies are) in order to engage in action that includes shared resistance, transformation, and globalized human agency.

Stink in rural communities doesn't come just from hog farms. In Prairie Town, the local ethanol plant generated a pungent odor that hung relentlessly in the air. We typically kept our doors and windows closed, even on nice warm days, in an effort to keep the smell outside. However, I'm not sure we were too successful in this. Nor were we alone. The recent emphasis on value-added agricultural products produced in rural areas, including turning corn into ethanol that can be added to gasoline and fuel oil, is a growing trend throughout rural communities. Of course, there is stink in urban areas too. Factories, smog, and pollution make air quality an issue in a variety of places throughout the world. The important question really is not about whether there is stink (in spite of "scientific" evidence to the contrary, we know it is there), but about whom decides who should live with it. Meanwhile, as the Bush administration froze or slowed down cleanup at thirty-three hazardous waste sites due to Superfund "shortchanges" and refusal on the administration's part to seek renewal of the industry tax, these pollutions and hazardous living conditions increasingly jeopardized the lives and well-being of individuals in nineteen states throughout the United States.[12]

These points raise important questions around issues of power and domination. In other words, someone or some group is always deciding how rural life should be; someone is in charge. The question is whether those decisions about the rural are arrived at collectively from the rural people in the community or whether someone else from outside the community is deciding. Neither power nor domination is ever static or complete. They are always circulating and changing. Whether there are overt symbols, like corn piles by the railroad tracks, or more subtle signs, like rust creeping across the water tower, people always "mediate and respond to the interface between their own lived experiences and structures of domination and constraint."[13] In other words, there is always resistance and power that moves among and across marginalized groups. We see it in Prairie Town where the Prairie Renaissance group has mobilized the community to change their lived conditions, and we see it throughout Pennsylvania where various groups are working to change state laws.

One of the ways in which local resistance can become more powerful is by linking up with others who share similar concerns through a shared agency that crosses the borders of our towns, states, countries. This agency can work to link rural individuals and groups together in order to find strength in unity. This work is difficult, as we'll see in what follows, but it seems worth the effort as it offers space for pedagogy that emphasizes learning through difference and a renewed sense of power and possibilities for collective change. In order to consider these possibilities, we'll look to recent U.S. farm policy and the consequences it has for rural people and countries worldwide.

Literacies That Cross the World

On May 13, 2002, George W. Bush signed the Farm Security and Rural Investment Act of 2002, just in time for primary elections in key agricultural states. According to a senior Republican official, Bush put aside earlier criticism that the bill locked in too much federal spending for too many years and that it would increase the disparity between large and small producers.[14] With primary elections occurring within days of the bill's signing, Bush knew that the one Senate seat needed for a Republican majority would likely come from a victory in one of the major farm states—South Dakota, Montana, Minnesota, Missouri, Iowa, or Georgia.[15] Meanwhile, the states that would reap the highest benefits from the bill, Iowa and Texas, were the home states of the agriculture committee chairmen for the House and Senate.[16] Bush's former rhetoric espousing devotion to the free market vanished as he continued his trend of contradicting campaign promises that called for fiscal responsibility and containment of government extravagance. The ten-year, $190 billion bill increased government support by $83 billion more than the cost of existing programs, a peculiar "budget buster" during a year when a $100 billion U.S. deficit was predicted.

Criticisms of the bill flared throughout the world. In the United States, conservatives complained the bill involved too much government spending. Others were outraged that two-thirds of the bill's subsidies will go to 10 percent of the farmers, continuing the trend of "welfare for the rich" that subsidized large-scale farms. Failed efforts to put lower caps on subsidies merely "watered down" the aid these farmers received.[17] Agriculture Secretary Ann Veneman voiced concern that the bill would encourage overproduction and jeopardize overseas markets.[18] Environmental activists complained that, in spite of the bill's provisions for grants to reduce manure run-off, the bill would jeopardize family farms because of its support for factory farms.

Abroad, the bill generated strong objections from the European Union, Canada, Australia, Brazil, and others who pointed out the hypocrisy of American farm policy that protected wealthy farmers from the market by guaranteeing particular prices in spite of what the market does, thus manipulating so-called "free trade." The anticipated vast oversupply of particular crops, coupled with record low prices and ever-larger subsidies to those farmers who produced the most more than threatened the well-being of countries that depended on agricultural exports. Canadian observers claimed the bill would drive Canadian farmers out of business, damage their economy, and make the country less self-sufficient in terms of food production.[19] In Latin and South American countries, the effects of the bill proved even more devastating. Brazilian experts estimated that the U.S. legislation would cost the country $2.4 billion in annual export revenues, while Chile anticipated a $1.5 billion loss per year. Guatemala, a country that relies on agricultural products for more than 75 percent of its gross domestic product, anticipated an even worse loss. Argentinian President Eduardo Duhalde stated, "We strongly condemn this move because the United States promotes free trade only when it suits them—later they change into obscene protectionists."[20]

Other countries, including Australia and members of the European Union, threatened to take charges against the United States to the World Trade Organization (WTO). The U.S. Farm Bill stood in stark contrast to the Doha Ministerial Declaration, discussed during a WTO public symposium just weeks before Bush signed the bill.[21] The declaration called for the establishment of a "fair and market-oriented trading system through a programme of fundamental reform" which included strengthened rules, and specific commitments for government support and protection for agriculture.[22] More significantly, the declaration, adopted on November 14, 2001, after input from 121 governments worldwide, stated the need to "correct and prevent restrictions and distortions in world agricultural markets."[23] Poor countries agreed to participate in this round of talks largely because the Bush administration promised that a top priority would be to phase out subsidies and engage in other practices that would increase access for poor countries in the world's agricultural markets.[24] Brazilian President Fernando Henrique Cardoso and other leaders of South American countries were angered that U.S. farm subsidies would jeopardize the Doha negotiations and further compromise developing countries given "special treatment" by the WTO. One senior World Bank official, who refused to be identified by name, was quoted as saying, "This is pretty galling . . . . A few American farmers will benefit, but at the expense of a very large number of poor people in developing countries."[25]

Decisions about farm policy made in the United States ripple consequences throughout the world. Third World[26] countries now must not only struggle against the double standards expressed in the conditions for "free trade" (i.e., U.S. markets won't purchase bruised fruit or vegetables and therefore will not buy fruit from Third World countries), they also must compromise their economic growth capacity to support a handful of rich American agribusinesses farmers. The farmers in these economically poor and struggling nations care little about the farm bill's provisions to help beginning farmers or to institute "country-of-origin" labeling, two facets of the bill that have been considered "good." Instead they will share abysmal experiences with small farmers in Prairie Town and other rural communities throughout the United States who are also marginalized through this policy.

The literacies in this situation and its potential consequences are multiple and competing. For those who approved passing this legislation in the United States, there is evidence of a literacy that reads capitalism as a "gospel of salvation."[27] Of course, capitalism in this case always includes a manipulation that protects the power and privilege of a few, while any explicitly expressed concern for globalization is merely an attempt to mask capitalism and to exercise power among the privileged. At the same time, the unbridled use of state power that is evidenced in the passage of this farm legislation is an act of domination that places the control of people's lives into the hands of a self-interested few. Such legislation, signed in spite of protest by people across the world, fails to even acknowledge the signs that point to the inevitable human suffering that will be perpetuated by the continued inequitable distribution of wealth and resources that extends throughout the world. Among the signs that are not read or even mentioned are the increasing number of people living in poverty in the United States and throughout the world, people who could not afford the cost of American food even if there is a vast oversupply. Nor does legislation and its backers acknowledge the number of children without health insurance or health care at a time when malnutrition among children, including American children, is a crisis. Although American farmers produce enough food to feed every person in the world daily,[28] there are still those who go hungry. The policy's protection of wealthy American farmers and agribusiness and the Bush administration's blatant disregard for earlier promises to the world that others would have the opportunity to engage in global free trade is sounding an alarm worldwide. Only a few share a literacy that reads value in the symbols this policy endorses—agribusiness, protection of the rich, consumption of natural resources, denial of basic needs to children and the poor. Instead, for the majority of farmers and others with rural interests, the policy is symbolic of the corrupt use of power driven by greed.

Others, particularly those who will suffer because of this policy, employ a literacy that recognizes the degree to which capitalism (i.e., greed) has failed to adequately solve the problems of people living under it. They see the dominant symbols of globalization, among them the WTO, the IMF, the World Bank, along with American foreign policy, and they read these texts against the lived experiences of themselves, their families, their neighbors, and realize there is no such thing as free trade, only domination of markets by people who have the most to lose in a material sense. Those who read injustices in this policy, particularly those who will suffer because of its consequences, can seize this opportunity to join with others across the world to resist. Those who believe there is value in local control of food production will find they share literacies with others across the world who no longer want to have food production controlled by a handful of American businesses. Such a new agrarian movement should be grounded in a literacy that interrogates the dominant symbols of these influences while simultaneously valuing open dialogue, choices, and having control of one's life. This literacy is situated in the sense that the *content* of the efforts for transformation may be different across the world. Farmers in India certainly face different situations than small U.S. farmers. However, the literacies in form are similar across place. These farmers read their rural way of life with eyes to similar signs—sometimes employing more traditional literacies, while other times employing neoliberal or new agrarian literacies. Recognition of the different ways in which we all come to read the world, and the similarities in the characteristics of these literacies, will open possibilities for joining hands with others to effect social transformation.

Of course, the hope to have open dialogue, choices, and more control over one's life is not limited to rural people or groups alone. In fact, there are many urban groups that share a similar literacy as they recognize the ways in which social and institutional structures have worked to alienate them. Recently, some have called for the formation of multiracial political coalitions that would cross urban areas into rural communities[29] to effect broad political change. Such an effort was initiated recently in Minnesota, and a brief discussion of this exchange in what follows will provide an example of the shared literacies and possibilities for bridging differences, in turn linking rural causes with others across the world who hope for the core characteristics of a new agrarian literacy.

Literacies That Bridge Differences

When we lived in Prairie Town, there was a Minnesota Public Radio four-part series that aired an exchange between residents of a small agricultural community just north of Prairie Town and people who gathered in a restaurant in Minneapolis. Crookston, the rural community, was made up largely of farmers who suffered significant losses during the farm crisis in the 1980s and extensive flooding throughout the Red River Valley in the 1990s. Those who gathered in Minneapolis met in a restaurant called "Lucille's Kitchen," known for its African American artifacts, soul food, and being "boldly black." The two groups were brought together because both constituencies seemed to feel they faced economic hard times, and both felt their voices were drowned out by their more powerful and affluent suburban neighbors. While there were vast differences in the populations represented by these two groups (the rural community consisted of approximately 8,000 people, mostly white, while Minneapolis had over 63,000 people representing a variety of nationalities and cultures), other demographic data was remarkably similar. The average per capita income for both groups hovered around $10,000, and unemployment was between 8 and 11 percent in both communities. The exchange between the two groups was interesting, to say the least, and careful review of their efforts points to some of the difficulties and possibilities political coalition-building can bring.

Initially, the two groups needed to spend time dispelling myths about one another, which included airing identity issues and some initial feelings of "I have it tougher than you." Rep. Gary Gray (DFL-Minneapolis), who attended the meetings, described one common misperception as "rural Minnesotans work, and work hard, but urban Minnesotans just have their hands out."[30] He expressed frustration with his feeling that Minnesotans rallied around rural and farm causes, but ignored the plight of those in the inner city. High school students from Minneapolis wondered aloud where kids in Crookston shopped and if they attended one-room schoolhouses, and Crookston teens wondered about the "crime and stuff" the inner city kids lived with and whether it was scary in their neighborhood.

Discussing issues of race brought some deep-seated tensions to the surface. One woman from St. Paul described how her daughter, an Ivy League law school graduate, was still followed around in stores, much like Prairie Town's economic advisor's daughter-in-law. She commented:

> Black people have found that it doesn't make any difference how much education people receive. They're still black people. . . . Don't tell me that what works for you, because you're white, will work for me—because I know it won't.[31]

Others in Lucille's Kitchen agreed, noting the fact that the farm crisis for white farmers is relatively new compared to the oppression their ancestors faced as slaves who worked on farms throughout the United States for generations.

Facilitators of the conversations broadcast between the two sites characterized the end result of the exchanges as a "search for similarities that turned up many differences."[32] However, in spite of the differences, the conversations brought about new understandings, particularly a consensus that racism and the farm crisis were the result of unfair and faulty systems. Both groups agreed the economic forces facing poor blacks and poor whites were similar. They ended the meetings by suggesting that a rural-urban alliance in the state would bring political power against the strength of suburban representation in the state government. Such an alliance will need to spread beyond these two groups to engage a range of communities in rural and urban areas in an organized and strategic effort to change policy in the state.

Of late, there have been a host of what some would have just years ago considered to be unlikely alliances. The seemingly unlikely unions of Turtles, Teamsters, and others that appeared on the streets of Seattle, Washington, D.C., Philadelphia, PA, Genoa, Italy, Montreal, and other cities[33] have generated hope that a people's movement could bring about social change. In spite of the possibilities these groups suggest, one common criticism of the political protests in Seattle and elsewhere is that the groups involved are disconnected and lack a nurturing and generous space that will allow radical ideas to take hold.[34] What Jonathan Rutherford, a member of the United Kingdom-based "Signs of the Times Group," has suggested is that sweeping oppositionalism alone is not enough; rather, efforts for resistance and change need to have objectives and to develop alternatives. Such resistance can materialize in a collective action that moves projects like the Crookston-Minneapolis exchange, the Prairie Renaissance project, the 10,000 Friends of Pennsylvania, and others into the foreground of rural life in ways that connect these individuals strategically to other groups. The common thread across all these groups, although it is not always explicitly mentioned as such, is a literacy that attends to the ways in which neoliberal influence has limited their choices and will work to further alienate them. Like those opposed to Bush's U.S. farm policy across the world, there are individuals and groups participating in these protests who read signs of U.S. domination of world policy, and want to transform such domination into a more democratic project that involves the participation of typically marginalized groups in the development of choices for themselves.

New Agrarian Literacies and Social Transformation

"Decent countries are made, not born," wrote historian Robin D.G. Kelley,[35] and the political struggles in which we engage do matter for they work to make the "stuff" of our democracy. While political coalitions are hopeful, in order for these "associations," as Kelley might refer to them, to continue, there needs to be a pedagogy, teaching and learning that change consciousness and link these groups to larger, globalized issues. Globalized in this sense points toward the need for the development of a group that shares consensus around interests and ideals. While there may be dissent around the details of their work together, the characteristics of their literacies, particularly the ways in which they read the dominant signs, would be unified and concerted for the sake of all humankind, thus enlarging the scope of freedom for individuals and groups across the world.[36] These groups and their resistance need to be more than passing images or sound bites, for it is within their activity that much hope for change and transformation that can bridge a variety of groups and peoples can be found. Iris Young's comments about the United States could be generalized to world contexts as she wrote:

> America is a big and complex society whose members have precious little shared experience other than what appears on their television screens. Only by listening to the voices of differently situated groups can a potential movement united for the sake of meeting people's needs have a clear sense of what those needs are.[37]

As the Crookston-Minneapolis exchanges suggested, it seems necessary and important to understand and embrace differences within a set of broader, unitary goals. Young continued:

> Unity and understanding for a new people's movement will not come from pretending that group differences do not matter, but rather from understanding precisely how they do matter, and so forging an inclusive picture of our social relations. We need to wake up to the challenge of understanding across difference rather than keep on dreaming about common dreams.[38]

To this time, there has been a lack of a credible vision for emancipatory progressive projects. Nancy Fraser noted that coalition politics, as they are currently conceptualized, remain "at the level of wishful thinking."[39] Over the past several decades, the Left has fallen prey to conflicting political interests that have worked to divide groups into unifocal interests that focus on specific causes but fail to link with others. The resulting lack of solidarity has meant that those who identify with some causes (for example, gay rights, feminist issues, etc.) fail to see how their efforts link with others who are similarly oppressed. There is no sense of solidarity, no shared literacy for liberation that unites groups in a progressive political movement. While many would likely agree with Fraser's observation, coalition and community-based projects embedded in a globalized public pedagogy that teaches us about ourselves and others and our shared ways of reading the world have the potential to move political groups beyond the stalemate that seems to currently exist. Moving political coalitions forward can happen with public engagement and pedagogy that embraces post-structuralist literacies that negotiate understandings, accommodate difference, and work toward a shared vision that embraces differences with the goal of transforming the world.

Political coalitions need to be conceptualized around literacy as a public globalized sphere that will provide the opportunity for radical societal pedagogy and change. In this sense, a public sphere is a space where citizenship can be redefined as the centerpiece of a struggle for social empowerment, where citizenship can cross geographic boundaries to engage in a unified movement for social justice. Both an active public engagement and civic courage are needed for this to be effective.[40] The public sphere of such a political coalition has the potential to explode myths and prejudices, a process that we saw beginning in the Crookston-Minneapolis exchange, and to challenge and redefine social issues that are prominent in today's society. An awareness of oppressive social forces as well as a commitment to engagement in the politics of daily life are needed as participants work simultaneously for cultural recognition and economic redistribution.[41] Further, focusing on compensatory issues alone is not enough; that is, there needs to be what Henry Giroux describes as an anticipatory language of "critical imagination" that will enable participants in critical, pedagogical projects such as political coalitions to:

[C]onsider the structure, movement, and opportunities in the contemporary order of things and how they might act to resist forms of oppression and domination while developing those aspects of public life that point to its best and as yet unrealized possibilities.[42]

Political coalitions that embrace a globalized public pedagogy can be conceptualized through a poststructural theoretical lens; that is, there needs to be an understanding that there is no single, clear river of history.[43] A poststructuralist lens will help participants in political coalitions to realize that meaning doesn't need to be given to them; instead, meaning can be achieved through "the struggles of a number of potential meanings and signifying practices."[44] Definitions of "community," "urban," "rural," "African American," "American," and other similar concepts need to be debated and redefined. Patrick Shannon noted that "For democracy to work, individuals must recognize that their identities are not fixed, abstract, or neutral."[45] That is, we must recognize that we can work to change the meanings that have been attributed to various aspects of our lives; we can change the way dominant symbols are read.

By learning about, critiquing, and redefining the current sociopolitical conditions, by employing a reflexive agency[46] that helps us to read and evaluate the conditions that face the poor and working poor across cultural groups in both urban and rural areas, there is the possibility that the world can be reshaped in a more equitable and just manner. Political coalitions must read the current conditions individuals are facing, employing a variety of literacies to understand the present, and then they must dare to dream of a different world. This dream must be the central point of any pedagogical work, rather than the cultural or class issues that need to be recognized but can work to divide. Ultimately our goal should be to work toward a reinvigorated democracy, one that will engage *all* citizens, regardless of race, class, gender, sexual orientation, or culture by making our personal struggles public matters. In this public transformative endeavor, there is the probability that we will all be changed.

In Prairie Town, as a new agrarian rural literacy begins to emerge, community members will begin this process as they connect to others throughout the world. Prairie Town's residents recognize, at least at some level, that the issues they face are social constructions that have ordered their lives, shaping their sense of reality and identity perhaps in ways they don't always choose. For many of us, it is difficult to imagine that life could be different. Prairie Town's story reminds us, however, that not everything can be bought and sold and perhaps more importantly that disidentification with societal structures and dominant discourses is possible within a participatory democratic society.

Continuing On

As we end this book, we're left with questions about what we might do. Arundhati Roy's expressed concern about the possibility for India and other developing countries to participate fully in the world's agricultural trade market will likely continue to be an issue in the next months and years as the WTO and nations worldwide work to negotiate the terms of "free trade" and the consequences it brings. Similarly, small communities throughout the United States, including Prairie Town, will need to wrestle with the contradictions and consequences this policy has for the few small farmers that remain in their communities and for a future where there may be few or no family farmers. In light of these somewhat bleak political and federal circumstances, it seems important for those who are in Prairie Town and similar communities to link their efforts to control the meanings and circumstances they face to others engaging in similar projects throughout the country and the world. In this way, we can take Arundhati Roy seriously as she called for a politics of resistance, "the politics of slowing things down . . . of joining hands across the world and preventing certain destruction."[47] As Prairie Town continues to connect its community first to itself and then labors to join hands with the country and other parts of the world, community members will find that they share literacies, resistances, and hopes with many other groups and individuals both nationally and internationally. Many other rural communities employ readings of rural life similar to those in rural Prairie Town, and it is to these similarities, to these possibilities for joining hands, that we must now turn our attention. This needs to become part of a broader political project that fights oppressive conditions in human life worldwide, for these conditions are not experienced in Prairie Town or rural communities alone. Capitalist ideologies have created human suffering through a disparate and asymmetrical power relation in which the vast majority of humans languish.

As people in Prairie Town struggle to make their own history, they do so with traditional and contemporary ways of reading the world. As they struggle to take the best of this past and incorporate it into a plan for the future, they will find their struggles link them to others throughout the world. My expectation is that they will continue on, carving out a political freedom that allows them to choose to live and work in the beauty of the rural American prairie. While this goal remains to be realized, as is true in any democratic project, there are conditions in place that should allow it to happen, not the least of which is the commitment by the people. Literacy is central to this work as we attempt to understand how people read the world and why, and as we find commonalities in these readings that allow us to link together across differences, across struggles, and across our dreams for a more just and equitable world.

Notes

Introduction

1. Neoliberalism is a political ideology that emphasizes market-based policies at the expense of social programs. Privatization, deregulation, and the dismantling of the welfare state characterize neoliberalism.

2. See Arundhati Roy, "Shall We Leave It to the Experts?" *The Nation*, February 18, 2002, 16-20.

3. Pierre Bourdieu, *The Weight of the World: Social Suffering in Contemporary Times* (Stanford: Stanford University Press, 1999), 382.

4. Roy, "Shall We Leave It?" 16.

5. "Prairie Town" is a pseudonym, as are all the names of residents interviewed in this book. "Prairie Town" refers to both the town and the nearby communities in the county where this study was conducted.

6. Paulo Freire and Donaldo Macedo, *Literacy: Reading the Word and the World.* (South Hadley, Mass.: Bergin and Garvey, 1987).

7. Henry Giroux, in Paulo Freire and Donaldo Macedo, *Literacy: Reading the Word and the World* (South Hadley, Mass.: Bergin and Garvey, 1987), 16.

8. Jason Sokol, "Solidarity on the Farm," *The Nation*, September 26, 2000, 6.

9. Liz Morrison, "Because of Government Infusion: Farm Financials Stable in [...] County," *"Prairie Town" Tribune*, March 16, 2000.

10. Prairie Town resident, personal interview, March 28, 2000.

11. David Fredrickson, "Fredrickson: Rural America's Future Hinges on People Speaking Up at Capitol," *"Prairie Town" Tribune*, March 16, 2000, 4B.

12. Lori Sturdevant, "On the Road Toward a New Rural Minnesota," *Minneapolis Star Tribune*, November 21, 1999, A23.

13. Peter Edelman, "Reforming Welfare-Take Two," *The Nation*, February 4, 2002, 16. Also see Deborah Connelly's *Homeless Mothers* (Minneapolis: University of Minne-

sota Press, 2000) for a detailed look at the lives of women and children directly impacted by Clinton's welfare reform policies.

14. Paul Theobald, *Teaching the Commons* (Boulder, Colo.: Westview Press, 1997).

15. See Kellogg Foundation, *Perceptions of Rural America*, 2002. At: www.wkkf.org/pubs/FoodRur/Pub2973.pdf

16. Ibid.

17. Theobald, *Teaching the Commons.*

18. See Jacqueline Edmondson, Greg Thorson, and David Fluegel, "Big School Change in a Small Town," *Educational Leadership* 57 (2000): 51–53, for a discussion of similar planning efforts that occurred in Herman, Minnesota.

19. The Blandin Foundation's mission is to strengthen rural Minnesota communities. Established in 1941, the foundation has a deep interest in rural towns and cities of the state. See www.blandinfoundation.org for more information.

20. I use "condition" here, rather than "crisis," to reflect Osha Gray Davidson's claims in *Broken Heartland: The Rise of America's Rural Ghettos* (Iowa City: University of Iowa Press, 1996), that the duration and extent of rural and agricultural struggles precipitates an ongoing condition rather than a short-lived crisis.

21. Pierre Bourdieu explained cultural capital as existing in three forms: the embodied state (i.e., long-lasting dispositions of the mind and body), the objectified state (i.e., cultural goods, including books, machines, movies, art), and the institutionalized state (i.e., universities and other societal institutions). See Pierre Bourdieu, "The Forms of Capital," in A. H. Halsey, Hugh Lauder, Phillip Brown, Amy Stuart Wells, eds., *Education: Culture, Economy, Society* (London: Oxford Press, 1997), 46-58.

22. William Greider, "The Last Farm Crisis," *The Nation*, November 20, 2000. 11-18.

23. Bourdieu, *Weight of the World*, 387.

24. It is interesting that agriculture has been characterized this way, given U.S. policies that historically have highly subsidized and regulated American farming.

25. In Jason Lina, "School District in Grant-writing Effort to Secure Funds for Long-range Planning," *"Prairie Town" Tribune*, July 27, 1999, A1.

26. See Eric T. Freyfogle, *The New Agrarianism: Land, Culture, and the Community of Life* (Washington, D.C.: Island Press, 2001).

27. Prairie Town resident, personal communication, March 8, 2000.

28. Roy, "Shall We Leave It?" 20.

29. Jacqueline Edmondson, *America Reads: A Critical Policy Analysis* (Newark, Del.: International Reading Association, 2000).

30. See Aronowitz and Giroux, 1993; Chall, 1996; Hirsch, 1988; Kozol, 1985; McQuillan, 1998; Shannon, 1998 for different perspectives on this crisis.

31. The Reading Excellence Act, passed into law in 1998, largely considered a Republican response to Clinton's America Reads Challenge program, specifically defined reading and research, in spite of an outcry by reading professionals that the definitions were too narrow. See Denny Taylor, *Beginning to Read and the Spin Doctors of Science* (Urbana, Ill.: NCTE, 1998) for one discussion of this legislation.

32. James Gee, *An Introduction to Discourse Analysis: Theory and Method* (New York: Routledge, 1999).

33. See Catherine McNicol Stock, *Rural Radicals* (New York: Beacon Press, 1996).

34. This will be discussed in more detail in chapter 5.

35. Ideology throughout this book is used in the sense described by Stanley Aronowitz. In *Science as Power: Discourse and Ideology in Education* (Minneapolis: University of Minnesota Press, 1988), Aronowitz argued that ideologies (rather than ideology) are a type of discourse with special languages, rules, and values that establish

parameters for our values and beliefs. However, he argued that ideologies are not completely determinate of people's understandings and beliefs, and the effects of ideologies are never completely predictable. There are conflicts and contradictions within ideologies, and as they compete to define truth, they often match the social, political, or economic power of the groups who accept them.

36. Mikhail Bahktin, *The Dialogic Imagination* (Austin: University of Texas Press, 1981).

37. James Gee, "Reading as Situated Language: A Sociocognitive Perspective. *Journal of Adolescent and Adult Literacy* 44 (2002): 720.

38. Bill Cope and Mary Kalantzis, *Multiliteracies: Literacy Learning and the Design of Social Futures* (London: Routledge, 2000), p. 5.

39. Ben Agger, *Fast Capitalism: A Critical Theory of Significance* (Chicago: University of Illinois Press, 1989), p. 51.

40. Stuart Hall, *Representation: Cultural Representations and Signifying Practices* (London: Sage, 1997).

41. See Alexander Stille, "Slow Food," *The Nation*, August 20, 2001.

42. Roger Simon, Claudia Eppert, Mark Clamen, and Laura Beres, "Witness as Study: The Difficult Inheritance of Testimony," *The Review of Education/Pedagogy/Cultural Studies* 22 (2001), 289.

43. Ibid., 295.

44. Glen Elder and Rand Conger, *Children of the Land: Adversity and Success in Rural America* (Chicago: University of Chicago Press, 2000), 52.

45. These other rural literacies are the subject of the next chapters.

46. In particular, consider Clinton's speech at the Pine Ridge Indian Reservation in South Dakota as one example (July 7, 1999).

47. Prairie Town resident, personal interview, February 24, 2000.

48. Thomas H. Benton, "Leaving the Big City for Small-Town College Life," *The Chronicle of Higher Education*, At: www.chronicle/com/jobs/2001/ 12/2001120301c.htm

49. Prairie Town resident, personal communication, January 18, 2000.

50. Mary Beth Lane. "Authorities Wary as Ohioan Takes over Aryan Nations," *The Columbus Dispatch*, October 3, 2001, 1B.

51. Lou Michel, "Unwelcome Guests: The Hate Group Aryan Nations Plans to Set Up Its New Headquarters in Ulysses, PA, a Two-hour Drive from Buffalo, and Residents Aren't Happy About Their New Neighbors, *The Buffalo News*, January 31, 2002, A1.

52. Agger, *Fast Capitalism*.

53. See Barry Yeoman, "Hispanic Diaspora," *Mother Jones*, July/August 2000; Eric Schlosser, "The Chain Never Stops," *Mother Jones*, July/August 2001.

54. Prairie Town resident, personal interview, February 24, 2000.

Chapter 1

1. Victor David Hanson, *The Land Was Everything: Letters from an American Farmer* (New York: Free Press, 2000).

2. Richard Shusterman, "France's Philosophe Impolitique," *The Nation*, May 3, 1999, 29.

3. Mark Steyn, "Sorry Mr. Bush, You've Lost Your Biggest Fan. Mark Steyn Says George Bush's Steel Tariffs are Grave Treachery," *Sunday Telegraph* (London), March 10, 2002, 22.

4. See Thomas Popkewitz, "The Denial of Change in Educational Change: Systems of Ideas in the Construction of National Policy and Evaluation," *Educational Researcher* 29 (2000): 17-29; Henry Giroux, "Rethinking Cultural Politics and the Radical Pedagogy in the Work of Antonio Gramsci," *Educational Theory* 49 (1999): 1-19.

5. See Deborah Connelly, *Homeless Mothers* (Minneapolis: University of Minnesota Press, 2000).

6. See Henry Giroux, "Zero Tolerance and Mis/education: Youth and the Politics of Domestic Militarization," *Tikkun*, March/April 2001: 29-35.

7. Jonathan Kozol, *Amazing Grace* (New York: Crown, 1995).

8. Henry Giroux, "Rethinking Cultural Politics and the Radical Pedagogy in the Work of Antonio Gramsci," *Educational Theory* 49 (1999): 1-19.

9. Jeremy Brecher, Tim Costello, and Brendan Smith, *Globalization From Below: The Power of Solidarity* (Cambridge, Mass.: South End Press, 2000).

10. Anderson, as cited in Brecher, Costello, and Smith, *Globalization From Below,* 7.

11. Perhaps the most common example of this was President Clinton asking Americans to subscribe to his values. He stated, "If you're willing to work hard and share our values, we'll join arm in arm with you and walk together into the future. You're part of our America" (August, 27, 1996).

12. Zygmunt Bauman, *The Individualized Society* (Cambridge: Polity Press, 2001).

13. Zygmunt Bauman, *Globalization: The Human Consequences* (New York: Columbia University Press, 1998).

14. W. K. Kellogg Foundation, *Perceptions of Rural America* (2002). At: www.wkkf.org/pubs/FoodRur/Pub2973.pdf.

15. Ibid.

16. Ibid., x.

17. Anne Rochester, *Why Farmers Are Poor: The Agricultural Crisis in the United States* (New York: International Publishers, 1940).

18. Katherine Skiba, "Kind is at Center of Farm Dispute; He Seeks More Funds for Conservation, Not Commodity Subsidies," *Milwaukee Journal Sentinal,* October 3, 2001, 3A.

19. William Julius Wilson, *The Bridge Over the Racial Divide* (Berkeley: University of California Press, 1999).

20. Jay Fonkert, "Changing Places: Shifting Livelihoods of People and Communities in Rural Minnesota," *Perspectives,* August 2001. At: www.mnplan.state.mn.us.

21. U.S. Department of Agriculture, as reported in ibid.

22. By "social capital," I mean the status, prestige, or respect that is needed to bring attention to these matters. Given conservative ideological influences in the United States, the poor are often considered to be failures because of their own shortcomings, whether intellectual, moral, or otherwise. Instead of attending to the voices of the poor, the public seems to largely hold them in disdain, an attitude that is further exacerbated by public policies that overtly label the poor as lazy, suggesting that jobs will rectify their plight.

23. See Donald Stull, Michael Broadway, and David Griffith, *Any Way You Cut It: Meat Processing and Small-town America* (Lawrence: University of Kansas Press, 1995).

24. See Osha Gray Davidson. *Broken Heartland: The Rise of American's Rural Ghetto* (Iowa City: University of Iowa Press, 1996).

25. Ibid.

26. This is not intended to be an all-encompassing definition of racism. For other views on racism, see Paul Gilroy's *Against Race* (Cambridge: Harvard University Press, 2000); Robin D.G. Kelley's *Yo Mama's Disfunktional* (Boston, Beacon Press, 1997);

William Julius Wilson's *The Bridge Over the Racial Divide* (Berkeley: University of California Press, 1999), among others.

27. Albert Memmi, *Racism* (Minneapolis: University of Minnesota Press, 2000), 169.

28. See Wilson, *Bridge Over the Racial Divide*.

29. Todd Lewan and Delores Barclay, *Torn From the Land*, Associated Press. At: www.timesunion.com/AspStories/story.asp?storyKey=72404&BCCode=TORN&newsda te=12/18/2001.

30. Stephen Bloom, *Postville: A Clash of Cultures in Heartland America* (New York: Harcourt, 2000).

31. See also Jeremy Ripkin, *Beyond Beef: The Rise and Fall of the Cattle Culture* (New York: Plume, 1992).

32. In 2001, Tyson Foods acquired IBP for $3.2 billion in cash and stock.

33. Barry Yeoman, "Hispanic Diaspora," *Mother Jones*, July/August, 2000, 33–41.

34. Ibid.

35. A neo-Nazi group.

36. Yeoman, "Hispanic Diaspora," 36.

37. The information on Iowa Beef Processors is based on a report by Eric Schlosser, "The Chain Never Stops," *Mother Jones,* July/August, 2001, 40–47.

38. See Stull et al.

39. As reported in Kirstin Downey Grimsely, "Tyson Foods Indicted in INS probe; U.S. Says Firm Bought Illegal Immigrants," *The Washington Post*, December 20, 2001, A01.

40. NAFTA (North American Free Trade Agreement), which went into effect January 1, 1994, opened up an unrestricted exchange of goods between the United States, Canada, and Mexico. The removal of tariffs on imported goods has had an effect on the food industry. For example, since NAFTA required the elimination of subsidies on Mexican corn crops, the price of Mexican corn rose to twice that of corn imported from the United States. Many in the United States opposed NAFTA, arguing that it would result in a loss of jobs for American citizens, but U.S. corporations justified NAFTA by arguing that moving their businesses abroad allows them to preserve jobs for U.S. workers. See Donald Stull, Michael Broadway, and David Griffith, *Any Way You Cut It: Meat Processing and Small-Town America* (Lawrence: University Press of Kansas, 1995) for a discussion of NAFTA's impact on the food industry.

41. Ibid.

42. Find living wage campaign information at www.epionline.org/livingwage/ index.cfm.

43. Yeoman, "Hispanic Diaspora."

44. in Stull et al., *Any Way You Cut It*.

45. Working conditions in the plant included strict rules about bathroom use, extreme heat, no windows or fans, verbal harassment of black workers by white supervisors, and old and faulty equipment. See Mary Tabor, "Poultry Plant Fire Churns Emotions Over Job Both Hated and Appreciated," *The New York Times*, September 6, 1991, A17.

46. Mary Tabor, "Poultry Plant Fire Churns Emotions Over Job Both Hated and Appreciated," *The New York Times*, September 6, 1991, A17.

47. Associated Press, "Victims of Poultry-Plant Fire to Get $16.1 Million," *The New York Times*, November 8, 1992, 40.

48. Ripkin, *Beyond Beef*.

49. See Stull et al., *Any Way You Cut It*; also see Barry Yeoman, "Hispanic Diaspora," *Mother Jones,* July/August, 2000, 33–41.

50. Ripkin, *Beyond Beef.*

51. David Griffith, "Hay Tabajo," in Stull, et al., *Any Way You Cut It,* 141.

52. Ibid.

53. Greg Thorson and Nicolas Maxwell, "Small Schools Under Siege: Evidence of Resource Inequality in Minnesota Schools," (Mankato, MN: Center for Rural Policy and Development, 2001).

54. Sandra Stalker, "Passing the test: Challenges and Opportunities in Rural Schools," *Perspectives,* August 2001. At: www.mnplan.state.mn.us.

55. Ibid.

56. Personal communication, March 29, 2000.

57. Personal communication, February 24, 2000.

58. Personal communication, February 24, 2000.

59. Albert Memmi, *Racism* (Minneapolis: University of Minnesota Press, 2000).

60. Henry Giroux, *Pedagogy and the Politics of Hope* (Boulder: Westview Press, 1997), 226.

61. Ibid.

62. Henry Giroux, "Public Pedagogy as Cultural Politics: Stuart Hall and the 'Crisis' of Culture," *Cultural Studies* 14 (2000): 352.

63. Iris Young, "The Complexities of Coalition," *Dissent* (1997): 65.

64. Ibid, 69.

Chapter 2

1. B. Sternberg, "What's the Future of Farming in Minnesota?" *The Star Tribune,* September 26, 1999.

2. These states include Wisconsin, Minnesota, North Dakota, South Dakota, and Montana. See Paul Gunderson's research as reported in *The Houston Chronicle,* November 3, 1991.

3. The Freedom to Farm Act was Republican-backed, and while President Clinton signed it into law, he expressed concern about the lack of safety nets for farmers. The Senate's Agriculture Committee at the time—which included Senators Santorum (PA), Daschle (SD), Harkin (IA), among others—was typical and tended to favor southern commodities and wheat.

4. It is important to note that this discussion treats the Freedom to Farm Act in very general terms. The legislation is large and complex, containing facets that are specific to the varied sectors of agriculture (from specific crop production to livestock and dairy policies). An in-depth treatment of each of these aspects of the legislation is not possible nor appropriate in this context. Instead, the intent is to provide an overview of farm policy that helps to situate the circumstances facing those living in Prairie Town and other agricultural-based communities at the outset of the twenty-first century.

5. E. Thomas McClanahan, "What Promise?" *The Kansas City Star,* June 4, 1996, B6.

6. Debbie Howlett and Richard Benedetto, "Under Old Policy, Little Control," *USA Today,* June 4, 1997, 2A.

7. David Hendee, "3rd District Candidate: Farmers Can't Have Freedom, Survival," *The Omaha World-Herald,* July 13, 2000, 26.

8. Howlett and Benedetto, "Under Old Policy."

9. See David Danbom, *Born in the Country: A History of Rural America* (Baltimore: Johns Hopkins University Press, 1995).

10. Guy Gugliotta, "Senate Passes $46 Billion Farm Bill; Fixed Payments Would Replace Crop Subsidies," *The Washington Post*, February 8, 1996, A1.

11. See *The Columbus Dispatch*, "Editorial and Comment," October 19, 1999, 10A.

12. See also Robert Reich, *The Future of Success* (New York: Knopf, 2000), for a discussion of anticipated changes in labor and work needs with globalization.

13. See Mary Neth, *Preserving the Family Farm: Women, Community, and the Foundations of Agribusiness in the Midwest, 1900–1940* (Baltimore: Johns Hopkins University Press, 1995).

14. See Danbom, *Born in the Country*.

15. President Nixon's Agriculture Secretary as quoted in Danbom, ibid., 255.

16. This point will be discussed more fully in chapter 3.

17. See Neth, *Preserving the Family Farm*.

18. Tom Meersman, "The Minnesota River in Crisis," *The Star Tribune*, December 12, 1999, 1R.

19. This is an area that has steadily improved since the 1940s after the Dust Bowl devastated large regions of the Midwest. However, attention to these issues is of concern to environmentalists.

20. As one example, Danbom pointed out that, in the United States, there is currently only one breed of chicken.

21. This is not to suggest that increasing the number of farmers would increase the diversity of crops and animals. Rather, the point is that modern farming is increasingly homogenous.

22. Greg Gordon, "Glickman Says Freedom to Farm Act Needs Fixing." *The Star Tribune*, January 11, 2000, 4A; *The Washington Post*, Editorial, May 30, 2000, A18.

23. See *Kansas City Star*, Opinion, April 28, 2000, B6.

24. As quoted in Tim Weiner, "Congress Agrees to $7.1 Billion in Farm Aid," *The New York Times*, April 14, 2000, A20.

25. See *Kansas City Star*, Opinion, April 28, 2000, p. B6.

26. See Danbom, *Born in the Country* for a more detailed explanation.

27. See Chris Clayton, "Family Farms Need Better Safety Net, Bradley Says," *The Omaha World Herald*, November 27, 1999, 1.

28. U.S. Department of Agriculture, February 29, 2000.

29. M. Schommer, "Agriculture Commissioner to Attend World Trade Organization Ministerial," *Minnesota Department of Agriculture Press Release*, November 29, 1999. At: www.mda.state.mn.us/DOCS/PRESSREL/99releas/Nov29_01.htm.

30. See U.S. Department of Agriculture, December 1999.

31. Paul Wellstone, "A 'Free Market' for Milk Pricing Would Wipe Out Our Dairy Industry," *The Star Tribune*, November 29, 1999, 13A.

32. U.S. Department of Agriculture, December 1999.

33. Tim Weiner, "Congress Agrees to $7.1 Billion in Farm Aid," *The New York Times*, April 14, 2000, A20.

34. Bill Clinton. Statement by the President on the farm bill signing, April 4, 1996, At: www.usda.gov/farmbill/state.htm.

35. Bill Clinton, Remarks by the President to the National Governors' Association, August 8, 1999, At: www.pub.whitehouse.gov/uri-res/I2R...:pdi:// oma. eop. gov. us /1999/8/10/16.text.1.

36. Judith Nygren, "Gore has Farmers on Mind, Small Producers Need Help, He Says," *The Omaha World Herald*, January 14, 2000, 7.

37. U.S. Department of Agriculture, *Agricultural Income and Finance: Situation and Outlook Report*. (Washington, D.C.: U.S. Government Printing Office, December 1999).

38. Bill Clinton, Remarks by the President in radio actuality on farm aid, July 31, 1999, At: www.pub.whitehouse.gov/uri-res/ I2R? urn: pdi: //oma. eop. gov. us /1999 /8 /2 /3.text.1.

39. Liz Morrison, "Because of Government Infusion: Farm Financials Stable in [...]County," *"Prairie Town" Tribune*, March 16, 2000, 1B.

40. Elizabeth Beeson and Marty Strange, *Why Rural Matters: The Need for Every State to Take Action on Rural Education* (Report prepared for the Rural School and Community Trust, 2000).

41. Stull et al., *Any Way You Cut It.*

42. Bill Clinton, Remarks to the LaCanasta Food Products Factory in South Phoenix, Arizona, July 7, 1999. At: www.whitehouse.gov/WH/library.html.

43. Stull et al., *Any Way You Cut It.*

44. Davidson, *Born in the Country*, 174.

45. Davidson, *Born in the Country.*

46. Davidson, *Born in the Country*, 175.

47. Personal communication, February 24, 2000.

48. Ibid.

49. Bill Clinton, Speech at Wyandotte, Mich., August 26, 1996, Washington, D.C.: Democratic Party press release.

50. Paul Wellstone, Keynote Address for Minnesota Association for Rural Telecommunications Annual Manager's Meeting, December 9, 1999. At: www.senate.gov /~wellstone /On_ the_ Record/Speeches_Articles/martspch.htm.

51. Personal communication, February 24, 2000.

52. Paul Wellstone, Keynote Address for Minnesota Association for Rural Telecommunications Annual Manager's Meeting. At: www.senate.gov /~wellstone /On_ the_ Record/Speeches_Articles/martspch.htm.

53. Personal communication, February 24, 2000.

54. See Neth, *Preserving the Family Farm.*

55. Personal communication, February 24, 2000.

56. Personal communication, March 8, 2000.

57. Governor's Strategic Planning Council, 2000. At: http://www. iowa2010.com.

Chapter 3

1. Kevin Brustuen, "Only the Hills Last Forever," *"Prairie Town" Sun Tribune*, May 25, 2000, 4.

2. These stories are drawn primarily from my visit to Prairie Town's historical museum, and I rely in large part on a booklet I purchased at the county museum. Written by Edna Mae Busch in 1976, it was an attempt to document the memories and events of the county, and it contains many stories gathered from local families.

3. See the introduction of this book for the definition of literacy operating here.

4. Written by Dorothy Darling Wagner in 1978 about her grandfather and their century farm. Given to me by Ms. Wagner's daughter.

5. See Jon Gjerde, *The Minds of the West* (Chapel Hill: University of North Carolina Press, 1997).

6. Faragher, 1986, as quoted in Paul Theobald, *Call School: Rural Education in the Midwest to 1918* (Carbondale: Southern Illinois University Press, 1995), 41.

7. Glen Elder and Rand Conger, *Children of the Land: Adversity and Success in Rural America* (Chicago: University of Chicago Press, 2000), 21.

8. See Kathleen Neils Conzen, "Peasant Pioneers: Generations Succession Among German Farmers in Frontier Minnesota." In Steven Hahn and Jonathan Prude, eds., *The Countryside in the Age of Capitalist Transformation: Essays in the Social History of Rural America* (Chapel Hill: University of North Carolina Press, 1985), 259-292.

9. See also Osha Gray Davidson, *Broken Heartland: The Rise of America's Rural Ghetto* (Iowa City: University of Iowa Press, 1996).

10. David Danbom, *Born in the Country: A History of Rural America* (Baltimore: John Hopkins University Press, 1995).

11. This is a myth. Family farms worked for some, but not for all, particularly the African American farmers discussed in chapter 2 of this book.

12. Mary Neth, *Preserving the Family Farm: Women, Community and the Foundations of Agribusiness in the Midwest, 1900-1940* (Baltimore: Johns Hopkins University Press, 1995), 18.

13. As quoted in Neth, *Preserving the Family Farm,* 237.

14. Edna Mae Busch, 5.

15. Edna Mae Busch.

16. Theobald, *Call School.*

17. Paul Theobald, *Teaching the Commons* (Boulder: Westview Press, 1997), 89.

18. John Mack Faragher, *Sugar Creek: Life on the Illinois Prairie* (New Haven: Yale University Press, 1986).

19. Theobald, *Teaching the Commons.*

20. This is a brief introduction to the various groups that organized in and around Prairie Town when the area was being settled. It is in no way meant to be a comprehensive statement about these groups.

21. Steven J. Keillor, *Cooperative Commonwealth: Co-ops in rural Minnesota 1859-1939* (St. Paul: Minnesota Historical Society Press, 2000), 5.

22. Theobald, *Teaching the Commons.*

23. Keillor, *Cooperative Commonwealth,* 5.

24. Ibid., 31.

25. Ibid., 32.

26. Theobald, *Teaching the Commons.*

27. Keillor, *Cooperative Commonwealth.*

28. See Rogers Smith, *Civic Ideals: Conflicting Visions of Citizenship in U.S. History* (New Haven: Yale University Press, 1997).

29. This characteristic sometimes drew criticism that the group was antirepublican. See Keillor, *Cooperative Commonwealth.*

30. Ibid.

31. Joint purchasing involved buying large quantities of products and supplies from wholesalers and manufacturers at a reduced rate. However, Grangers' lack of solidarity contributed to suspicion and controversy among members. See ibid.

32. See Danbom, *Born in the Country.*

33. Edna Mae Busch.

34. Keillor, *Cooperative Commonwealth.*

35. Ibid., 153.

36. Catherine McNichol Stock, *Rural Radicals: From Bacon's Rebellion to the Oklahoma City Bombing* (New York: Penguin Books, 1996).

37. Ibid.

38. See the Minnesota Democratic-Farmer-Labor Party Platform. At: www.dfl.org.

39. This is in contrast to the Farm Bureau, in particular, which was organized in a top-down fashion and aligned with the federal government. The Farm Bureau is dis-

cussed in more detail later in this chapter. It is not included here because it was not a grassroots movement.

40. Neth, *Preserving the Family Farm,* 209.

41. I use the term "pedagogy" consistent with Henry Giroux's explanation of critical, public pedagogy. In other words, pedagogy "is about the intellectual, emotional, and ethical investments we make as part of our attempt to negotiate, accommodate, and transform the world in which we find ourselves" (1997, p. 226). Giroux notes that the pedagogical is a defining principle of cultural politics.

42. Edna Mae Busch.

43. Churches played a large role in the English language education of immigrant populations.

44. Edna Mae Busch, 117.

45. Theobald, *Call School,* 73-74.

46. Edna Mae Busch.

47. As quoted in Jon Gjerde, *The Minds of the West* (Chapel Hill: University of North Carolina Press, 1997), 322.

48. Ibid.

49. Theobald, *Call School.*

50. Because of hopes to assimilate Native Americans into the dominant discourses of American culture, as well as accompanying policies around the exclusiveness of language, ethnicity, and culture, Indian Schools were formed throughout the country. These schools and the federal policies that created them were directed toward comprehensive national education of Native Americans in the United States. In particular, the General Allotment Act of 1887 and President Grant's "peace policy" tried to destroy tribal relations and assimilate Native Americans into the mainstream American culture through education and displacement from their native lands. Shifts in federal policy, in this case the first being the shift from a contract with the Catholic church and the Sisters of Mercy to complete federal control in an effort to keep church and state separate, followed by efforts to shift the schools to state control, led to the closing of the Indian schools. Any state government that took over former Indian school buildings needed to provide education to Native American students tuition free, but there was no guarantee that Native Americans would seek education in these locales—they were removed from their families and tribes, and they typically devalued the Native American cultures. By 1910, Indian schools were largely a thing of the past. See Bert Ahern, "Indian Education and Bureaucracy: The School at [Prairie Town] 1887-1909," *Minnesota History* (1984), 82-98, for more information on this particular school.

51. Theobald, *Teaching the Commons,* 15.

52. Prairie Town resident, March 28, 2000, personal communication.

53. See D. Clausen, *Prairie Son* (Minneapolis, Minn.: Mid-List Press, 1999) or M. Douglas, *Eggs in the Coffee, Sheep in the Corn: My Seventeen Years as a Farm Wife* (St. Paul: Minnesota Historical Society Press, 1994) for autobiographies of two families' struggles to sustain a life on farms near Prairie Town during this time.

54. Ferdinand Tonnies, *Community and Society* (New York: Harper and Row. 1887/1963).

55. Ian Hughes, "Gemeinschaf & Gesellschaft," *Community and Study Knowledge Base* (2000). At: www.cchs.usyd.edu.au/bach/pub/community/ g&g.htm.

56. Ferdinand Tonnies, "The Concept of Gemeinschaft," in W.J. Cahnman and R. Herberle, eds., *Ferdinand Tonnies on Sociology: Pure, Applied and Empirical. Selected Writings,* 62-72 (Chicago: University of Chicago Press, 1925), 69.

57. See Larry Lyon, *The Community in Urban Society* (Prospect Heights, Ill.: Waveland, 1999) for a clear explanation of these distinctions.

58. Ibid.

59. Danbom, *Born in the Country,* 167.

60. Report of the Commission on Country Life, 1944, as quoted in Paul Theobald, *Teaching the Commons* (Boulder: Westview Press, 1997), 103.

61. Danbom, *Born in the Country,* 170.

62. Theobald, *Teaching the Commons.*

63. Ibid., 105-106.

64. See Elder and Conger, *Children of the Land.*

65. Neth, *Preserving the Family Farm.*

66. Ibid., 133.

67. Ibid., 130.

68. See ibid. See also Stock, *Rural Radicals.*

69. See Mary Neth, *Preserving the Family Farm.*

70. Ibid., 134.

71. Stock, *Rural Radicals.*

72. See the American Farm Bureau Federation. At: www.fb.org.

73. See *Amber Waves of Gain: How the Farm Bureau is Reaping Profits at the Expense of America's Family Farmers, Taxpayers, and the Environment,* April, 2000. At: www.defenders.org/fb/awg01.pdf.

74. Ranked by *Fortune Magazine,* as reported on the Minnesota Farm Bureau home page. At: www.minnesotafarmbureau.org.

75. Information on legislation was obtained from the *Amber Waves of Gain* report.

76. Neth, *Preserving the Family Farm,* 6.

77. Theodore Caplow and Howard Bahr, *Middletown Families: Fifty Years of Change and Continuity* (Minneapolis: University of Minnesota Press, 1982), 5.

78. Stanley Aronowitz, *Science as Power: Discourse and Ideology in Modern Society* (Minneapolis: University of Minnesota Press, 1988).

Chapter 4

1. Ray Marshall and Marc Tucker, *Thinking for a Living: Work, Skills, and the Future of the American Economy* (New York: Basic Books, 1992), xvi.

2. This should not be considered an indictment of Burger King. Rather, it is an example, one of many, that demonstrates the influence of society on rural communities and the questions that heightened capitalism brings.

3. Burger King's trademarked corporate slogan.

4. R. Pannu, "Neoliberal Project of Globalization: Prospects for Democratization of Education," *Alberta Journal of Education* 42 (1996): 87-101.

5. Ibid., 93.

6. A. Boron and C. Torres, "The Impact of Neoliberal Restructuring on Education and Poverty in Latin America," *Alberta Journal of Education* 42 (1996): 102-114.

7. This was discussed in greater detail in chapter 2 of this book. The most common proposals for solving the "problems" of rural communities have involved providing more jobs for the region, particularly meat packing plants and telecommunications industries.

8. This is not meant to suggest that more centralized and standardized education was any better equipped to meet global marketplace needs. In spite of this, throughout the 1990s, education was promoted as necessary toward this goal.

9. Zymunt Bauman, *Community: Seeking Safety in an Insecure World* (New York: Polity Press, 2001), 41-42.

10. See Paul Theobald, *Teaching the Commons* (Boulder: Westview Press, 1997).

11. See Noam Chomsky, *Profit over People: Neoliberalism and the Global Order* (New York: Seven Stories Press, 1999).

12. Although contracts have been used in agriculture since the early 1900s, the frequency and extent of use have risen sharply since the 1950s, particularly in the poultry and pork industries. Steve Martinez reported that independent growers raised 95 percent of broilers (chicken used for meat rather than eggs) in 1950. By 1955, only 10 percent were independently raised, while 88 percent involved contractual agreements and 2 percent involved integrator-owned arrangements. See Steven W. Martinez, "Price and Quality of Pork and Broiler Products: What's the Role of Vertical Coordination?" *Current Issues in the Economics of Food Markets* (Washington, D.C.: Economic Research Service, U.S. Department of Agriculture, February 2000).

13. Economic Research Service, U.S. Department of Agriculture, "Farm structure: glossary." At: www.ers.usda.gov/briefing/farmstructure/contract. Htm.

14. Economic Research Service, U.S. Department of Agriculture, "Farmers' Use of Marketing and Production Contracts." At: www.ers.usda. gov/publications/aer74701/.

15. Prairie Town resident, personal communication, March 28, 2000.

16. Ibid.

17. Martinez, "Price and Quality of Pork and Broiler Products."

18. Ibid., 1.

19. See chapter 2 for more information on recent farm policies.

20. Of course even American made cars have foreign parts and services.

21. Bauman, *Community*, 8.

22. Ibid., 14 (italics in original).

23. Ibid., 29.

24. Ibid., 92.

25. Ibid., 93.

26. Bill Clinton. Speech at Wyandotte, Mich., August 28, 1996. Washington, D.C.: Democratic Party Press Release.

27. Frances Fowler, "The Neoliberal Value Shift and Its Implications for Federal Education Policy Under Clinton," *Educational Administration Quarterly* 31 (1995): 38-60.

28. Robert Reich, as cited in Fowler, "The Neoliberal Value Shift," 48.

29. David Sehr offers an understandable distinction between private and public democracy in *Education for Public Democracy* (New York: SUNY Press, 1997).

30. Robert Reich, *The Future of Success* (New York: Knopf, 2000), 196.

31. See Bauman, *Community*.

32. Stanley Aronowitz and Henry Giroux, *Education Still Under Siege* (Westport, Conn.: Bergin and Garvey, 1993), 59.

33. Reich, *The Future of Success*.

34. Elder and Conger, *Children of the Land*.

35. This is not to suggest that these core values were not problematic, particularly those that worked to institutionalize racism.

36. See also Bloom, *Postville*.

37. This will be discussed in great detail in chapter six.

38. See Theobald, *Call School*. While some, including those like the Country Life Movmement, may espouse education as contributing to the enhancement of life in rural communities, others see such endeavors as contributing to its decline, particularly as young people increasingly move away from rural towns for work in the city.

39. Toni Haas and Paul Nachitgal, *Place Value: An Educator's Guide to Good Literature on Rural Lifeways, Environments, and Purposes of Education* (Charleston, West Va.: ERIC Clearinghouse on Rural Education and Small Schools, 1998), 5.

40. See Jacqueline Edmondson and Patrick Shannon, "Reading Education and the 21st Century: Questioning the Reading Success Equation," *Peabody Journal of Education* 73 (1999): 104-126.

41. Marshall Smith and Brent Scoll, "The Clinton Human Capital Agenda" *Teachers College Record* 96 (1995): 389-404.

42. Marshall and Tucker, *Thinking for a Living*; Peter Sacks, *Standardized Minds* (New York: Perseus Books, 1999).

43. Sacks, *Standardized Minds*; Susan Ohanian, *One Size Fits Few* (Portsmouth, N.H.: Heinemann, 1998).

44. Alex Molnar, *Giving Kids the Business: The Commercialization of America's Schools* (Boulder: Westview Press, 1995).

45. Kozol, *Amazing Grace*.

46. Clinton, August 28, 1996.

47. Paul Nachtigal, *Rural Education: In Search of a Better Way* (Boulder: Westview Press, 1982).

48. These state tests are required for graduation. See Norman Draper, "One Third of Black 11th Graders Have Flunked State Tests," *Minneapolis Tribune,* April 28, 1999, for an analysis of test results by race.

49. See Jason Tina, "Long-range Planning Looks at Fundraisers, Alternatives to I hem," *"Prairie Town" Sun Tribune,* December 2, 1999, 1–2.

50. Strategic Plan for the "Prairie Town" Area School District, 2000, 15.

51. As defined by Fowler.

52. See Patrick Shannon and Jacqueline Edmondson, "A Look at Educational Benchmarking in the United States," *Curriculum Perspectives* 18(3) (1998): 45–49 for a discussion of the New Standards Project.

53. This is not intended to be a comprehensive discussion of standardization in schools. Rather, it is intended to consider the complications of standardization in rural Prairie Town.

54. Jacqueline Edmondson, "Taking a Broader Look: Reading Literacy Education Reform," *The Reading Teacher* 54 (6) (2001): 620–628.

55. For a discussion of centralization/decentralization, see Thomas Popkewitz, "The Denial of Change in Educational Change: Systems of Ideas in the Construction of National Policy and Evaluation," *Educational Researcher* 29 (2000): 17-29.

56. The graduation standards technicians were often practicing teachers who had received some extra training from the state about the graduation standards. Some had a one year sabbatical from their teaching, which allowed them to travel to various schools to assist with writing performance packages and teacher training. Others facilitated the work of teachers in their own schools as they continued with their regular teaching responsibilities.

57. Minnesota funds its schools based on a per pupil formula. As populations decrease, so does the available money for schools. During the time of this study, efforts were made to change the funding situation for small and rural schools by introducing a "small school" allotment to the state's complex formula. A report of this effort can be found in Greg Thorson and Jacqueline Edmondson, *Making Difficult Times Worse: The Impact of per Pupil Funding Formulas on Rural Minnesota Schools.* Report written for the Center for Rural Policy, Minnesota State University, Mankato, Minn., 1999.

58. Fifth grade teacher, personal communication, February 8, 2000.

59. Sixth grade teacher, personal communication, March 7, 2000.

60. Second grade teacher, personal communication, January 18, 2000.

61. See also Edmondson, "Taking a Broader Look."

62. First grade teacher, personal communication, January 18, 2000.

63. Prairie Town school librarian, personal communication, March 9, 2000.

64. Bob Buresh, "School District Organizational Alternatives: Background and Available Information," At: cfl.state.mn.us/FACILIT/orgalt.html.

65. See Jacqueline Edmondson, Greg Thorson, and David Fluegel, "Big School Change in a Small Town," *Educational Leadership,* 57 (7) 2001: 51– 53, for the story of a neighboring town's efforts to keep its school.

66. Fifth grade teacher, personal communication, February 8, 2000.

67. Henry Giroux, *Teachers as Intellectuals* (Westport, Conn.: Bergin and Garvey, 1988).

68. See Bill Clinton, "State of the Union Address," February 28, 1997. At: www.whitehouse.gove/WH/library.html.

69. Nicholas Lemann, *The Big Test* (New York: Farrar, Strauss, and Giroux, 1999), 6.

70. Interestingly enough, less than 5 percent of the total enrollment at the nearby University of Minnesota campus consists of Prairie Town graduates. The majority of these students go to other areas for their post-secondary education.

71. Alan DeYoung. "Children at Risk in America's Rural Schools: Economic and Cultural Dimensions," In R. Rossi, ed., *Schools and Students at Risk: Context and Framework for Positive Change* (New York: Teachers College Press, 1994), 249.

72. See Kenneth Gray, *Getting Real: Helping Teens Find Their Future.* (Thousand Oaks, Calif.: Corwin Press, 2000), 3.

73. See George W. Bush's education plan "No Child Left Behind" as one example.

74. First grade teacher, personal communication, December 20, 1999.

75. Reich, *The Future of Success,* 202.

76. Prairie Town parent, personal communication, March 20, 2000.

77. Charles Lemert, *Social Things* (Lanham, Md.: Rowman & Littlefield, 1997).

78. Jan Nespor, *Tangled Up In School* (Mahwah, N.J.: Lawrence Erlbaum, 1991).

79. Nespor, *Tangled Up In School,* 169.

80. Colin Lankshear, *Changing Literacies* (Buckingham: Open University Press, 1997), 30.

81. Brian Street, *Social Literacies* (London: Longman, 1995), 127.

82. James Gee, Glynda Hull, and Colin Lankshear, *The New Work Order* (Boulder: Westview, 1996).

83. Marshall Berman, *Adventures in Marxism* (New York: Verso, 1999), 101.

84. See Smith and Scoll, "The Clinton Human Capital Agenda."

85. See Reich, *The Future of Success,* particularly for a discussion of sorting mechanisms.

86. Reich, *The Future of Success.*

87. Pierre Bourdieu, *Acts of Resistance* (New York: New Press, 1998), 110.

Chapter 5

1. Alain Badiou, *Ethics: An Essay on the Understanding of Evil* (London: Verso, 2001).

2. Jason Lina, "Parents Say They Want Basics, Not Controversy," *The "Prairie Town" Sun Tribune,* April 17, 2002.

3. Ibid.

4. Ibid.

5. Ibid.

6. Minnesota's public school funding was discussed in chapter 4. Briefly, districts received an allotment for each child enrolled in its schools.

7. For a discussion of institutional power and surveillance, see Michel Foucault, *Power/knowledge: Selected Interviews and Other Writings, 1972-1977* (New York: Pantheon Press, 1980).

8. Thanks to David Fluegel for this information.

9. See the Blandin Foundation website at www.bclp.org/build.html

10. Blandin has trained more than 3,000 community leaders from over 200 rural communities.

11. Personal communication, March 8, 2000.

12. Personal communication, February 24, 2000.

13. Philip Drown, "[Prairie Town] and Surround Area/Blandin Community Investment Partnership Process Narrative, Prepared for BCIP Steering Committee," May 15, 2000. At: mrs.umn.edu/academic/fclt/bcipnarrative.html.

14. See Roger Simon, in Patrick Shannon, *Becoming Political Too* (Portsmouth, N.H.: Heinemann, 2001).

15. Drown, "[Prairie Town] and Surrounding Area/Blandin Community Investment Partnership Process Narrative "

16. Ibid.

17. Philip Drown, Grant Monitoring Report: Prairie Renaissance Project, March 1, 2001, 2.

18. Drown, "[Prairie Town] and Surrounding Area/Blandin Community Investment Partnership Process Narrative."

19. David Sehr, *Education for Public Democracy* (New York: SUNY Press, 1997), 77–78.

20. Paul Theobald, *Call School* (Boulder: Westview Press, 1997).

21. Zygmunt Bauman, *Community* (Cambridge: Polity Press, 2001), 19.

22. Amy Burke, "Patriotism and Community," *Dissent* (Spring 2002), 45.

23. Karl Marx, as explained by Marshall Berman, *Adventures in Marxism* (New York: Verso, 1999).

24. Imre Szeman, "Introduction: Learning to Learn from Seattle," *The Review of Education, Pedagogy, and Cultural Studies* 24 (2002): 1–12.

25. Brian Street, *Social Literacies* (London: Longman, 1995), 6.

26. Herbert Marcuse, *One Dimensional Man* (New York: Beacon, 1964).

27. Henry Giroux, "Public Pedagogy as Cultural Politics: Stuart Hall and the 'Crisis of Culture,'" *Cultural Studies* 14 (2000): 341-360, 355.

28. See Chantal Mouffe, "Radical Democracy or Liberal Democracy," In David Trend, ed., *Radical Democracy* (New York: Routledge, 1996), 19-26.

29. See also Bill Cope and Mary Kalantzis, *Multiliteracies* (London: Routledge, 2000).

30. Charles Lemert, *Social Things* (Lanham, Md.: Rowman and Littlefield, 1997).

31. Berman, *Adventures in Marxism*, 99.

32. See also Cope and Kalanztis, *Multiliteracies*.

33. See Robert Reich, *The Future of Success* (New York: Knopf, 2000) for a discussion of success in the new economy.

Chapter 6

1. The town is close enough to an interstate highway that drug trafficking has become a lucrative source of income for some.

2. Thomas Alan Lindzey, "Policies That Matter for Family Farmers," *Centre Daily Times*, May 1, 2002, A10.

3. Thomas A. Linzey, "Senate Spreads Sludge," *Scranton Times Tribune*, May 6, 2002.

4. Associated Press, "Suit Over Hog Farm Odor is Settled in Illinois Case," *St. Louis Dispatch*, May 8, 2002, B3.

5. Tim Bryant, "Cargill Pork Will Pay $1 Million Fine Plus Costs for Illegal Dumping of Waste," *St. Louis Post-Dispatch*, February 20, 2002, C8.

6. Enron and Worldcom are but two of many contemporary examples of the human suffering caused by this lack of ethics.

7. Tom Spears, "Pig Farm Neighbours Win Property Tax Cuts: Ontario, Alberta Rule Factory Farms Damage Value of Surrounding Land," *The Ottawa Citizen*, March 28, 2002, A5.

8. Tom Spears, "Why Canada Is Becoming a Nation of Pigs: Exploding Growth in Factory Hog Farms Sets Farmers Against Neighbours Who Are Worried About Pollution," *The Ottawa Citizen*, March 27, 2002, A1.

9. Christopher Mele, *Selling the Lower East Side: Culture, Real Estate, and Resistance in New York City* (Minneapolis: University of Minnesota Press, 2000), 17.

10. Imre Szeman, "Introduction: Learning to Learn from Seattle." *The Review of Education, Pedagogy, and Cultural Studies*, 24 (2002), 1-2: 3.

11. Mele, *Selling the Lower East Side*, 20.

12. See "Shortchanged Superfund," *Boston Globe*, July 8, 2002, A10; Christine Todd Whitman, "Keep the Momentum for Superfund Cleanups," *New York Times,* July 18, 2002, 21.

13. Henry Giroux, *Theory and Resistance in Education: Toward a Pedagogy for the Opposition* (Westport, Conn.: Bergin & Garvey, 2001), 108.

14. Mike Allen, "Bush Signs Bill Providing Big Farm Subsidy Increases," *The Washington Post,* May 13, 2002, A01.

15. Allen, "Bush Signs Bill Providing Big Farm Subsidy Increases."

16. Edward Alden and Deborah McGregor, "A Cash Crop: The US Farm Bill Has Upset other countries by reversing past efforts to encourage agricultural free trade," *The Financial Times Limited, London*, May 10, 2002, 18.

17. Tiffany Ray, "Recently Passed Farm Bill Draws Mixed Reactions," *The Topeka Capital Journal*, May 10, 2002.

18. Allen, "Bush Signs Bill Providing Big Farm Subsidy Increases."

19. Sun News Services, "Bush Plants $190B Farm Bill," *The Edmonton Sun*, May 14, 2002, 46.

20. Agence France Press, "Latin America Vows to Fight US Farm Bill," *Agence Free Press*, May 14, 2002, Financial pages.

21. The Doha WTO public symposium was held April 29–May 1, 2002. More information on this symposium and the full text of the Doha Ministerial Declaration can be found at www.wto.org.

22. Doha Declaration Explained, At: www.wto.org/english/tratop_e/dda_e/dohaexplained_e.htm.

23. Ibid.

24. Paul Blustein, "US Farm Bill Finds Few Fans Abroad: Increased Subsidies Flout Consensus on Helping Third World Agriculture," *The Washington Post*, May 5, 2002, A24.

25. Blustein, "US Farm Bill Finds Few Fans Abroad."

26. I must note here that I despise the term "Third World" and use it only because there is a shared general understanding among the audience for this text of which countries constitute "Third World" nations. My use of this term in no way indicates that the peoples or countries it refers to are of lesser quality than "First World" nations.

27. Jean Camaroff and John L. Camaroff, "Millennial Capitalism: First Thoughts on a Second Coming," *Public Culture* 12 (2), 292.

28. Nespor, *Food Politics.*

29. See William Julius Wilson, *The Bridge over the Racial Divide* (Berkley: University of California Press, 1999).

30. David Peterson, "Rural/urban Forum Yields Agreement, Obstacles," *Minneapolis Star Tribune*, March 24, 1999.

31. David Hawley, "Distant Communities Find Common Ground," *St. Paul Pioneer Press*, February 10, 1999, C1 & C4.

32. David Peterson, "Differences Still Outweigh Similarities in Last Broadcast of Rural-urban Talks." *Minneapolis Star Tribune*, April 21, 1999.

33. See Imre Szeman, "Introduction," *The Review of Education, Pedagogy and Cultural Studies*, 24 (2002), 1-2: 1-12.

34. See Jonathan Rutherford, "After Seattle," *The Review of Education, Pedagogy and Cultural Studies*, 24 (2002), 1-2: 13-27.

35. Robin D.G. Kelley, *Yo Mama's Dysfunktional* (New York: Beacon, 1997), 101.

36. See Marshal Berman, *Adventures in Marxism* (New York: Verso, 1999).

37. Iris Young, "The Complexities of Coalition." *Dissent*, Winter 1997, 68.

38. Young, "The Complexities of Coalition," 69.

39. Nancy Fraser, *Justice Interruptus* (New York: Routledge, 1997).

40. See Henry Giroux, *Theory and Resistance in Education:Toward a Pedagogy for the Opposition* (Westport, Conn.: Bergin & Garvey, 2001).

41. See Wendy Morgan, *Critical Literacy in the Classroom: The Art of the Possible* (New York: Routledge, 1997) and Fraser, *Justice Interruptus.*

42. Henry Giroux, *Impure Acts: The Practical Politics of Cultural Studies* (New York: Routledge, 2000), 34-35.

43. See Morgan, *Critical Literacy.*

44. See Morgan, *Critical Literacy*, 8.

45. Patrick Shannon, "Fattening Frogs For Snakes," in Larson, ed., *Literacy for Sale* (New York: Peter Lang, 2001), 23.

46. Shannon, "Fattening Frogs for Snakes."

47. Arundhati Roy, "Shall We Leave It To The Experts?" *The Nation*, February 18, 2002, 20.

References

Agence France Press, "Latin America vows to fight US Farm Bill." *Agence Free Press,* May 14, 2002, Financial pages.

Agger, Ben. *Fast Capitalism: A Critical Theory of Significance.* Chicago: University of Illinois Press, 1989.

Alden, Edward, and McGregor, Deborah. "A cash crop: The US farm bill has upset other countries by reversing past efforts to encourage agricultural free trade." *The Financial Times Limited, London,* May 10, 2002, p. 18.

Allen, Mike. "Bush Signs Bill Providing Big Farm Subsidy Increases." *The Washington Post,* May 13, 2002, p. A01.

Aronowitz, Stanley. *Science as Power: Discourse and Ideology in Education.* Minneapolis: University of Minnesota Press, 1988.

———, and Henry Giroux. *Education Still Under Siege.* Westport, Conn: Bergin and Garvey, 1993.

Associated Press. "Victims of Poultry-Plant Fire to Get $16.1 Million." *The New York Times,* November 8, 1992, p. 40.

Associated Press. "Suit over hog farm odor is settled in Illinois Case." *St. Louis Dispatch,* May 8, 2002, p. B3.

Badiou, Alain. *Ethics: An Essay on the Understanding of Evil.* London: Verso, 2001.

Bahktin, Mikhail. *The Dialogic Imagination.* Austin: University of Texas Press, 1981.

Bauman, Zygmunt. *Globalization: The Human Consequences.* New York: Columbia University Press, 1998.

———. *Community: Seeking Safety in an Insecure World.* New York: Polity Press, 2001.

———. *The Individualized Society.* Cambridge: Polity Press, 2001.

Beeson, Elizabeth, and Marty Strange. *Why Rural Matters: The Need for Every State to Take Action on Rural Education.* Report prepared for the Rural School and Community Trust, 2000.

Benton, Thomas H. "Leaving the Big City for Small-Town College Life," *The Chronicle of Higher Education.* At: www.chronicle/com/jobs/2001/12/ 2001120301c.htm.

Berman, Marshall. *Adventures in Marxism.* New York: Verso, 1999.

Bloom, Stephen. *Postville: A Clash of Cultures in Heartland America.* New York: Harcourt, 2000.

Blustein, Paul. "US Farm Bill Finds Few Fans Abroad: Increased Subsidies Flout Consensus on Helping Third World Agriculture." *The Washington Post*, May 5, 2002, p. A24.

Boron, Atilio, and Carlos Torres."The impact of neoliberal restructuring on education and poverty in Latin America." *Alberta Journal of Education 42* (1996): 102-114.

Boston Globe. "Shortchanged Superfund." July 8, 2002, p. A10.

Bourdieu, Pierre. "The Forms of Capital." in A. H. Halsey, Hugh Lauder, Phillip Brown, Amy Stuart Wells, eds. *Education: Culture, Economy, Society* (London: Oxford Press, 1997), pp. 46-58.

————. *Acts of Resistance.* New York: The New Press, 1998.

————. *The Weight of the World: Social Suffering in Contemporary Times.* Stanford: Stanford University Press, 1999.

Brecher, Jeremy, Tim Costello, and Brendan Smith. *Globalization from Below: The Power of Solidarity.* Cambridge, Mass.: South End Press, 2000.

Brustuen, Kevin. "Only the Hills Last Forever." *"Prairie Town" Sun Tribune*, May 25, 2000, A4.

Bryant, Tim. "Cargill Pork Will Pay $1 Million Fine Plus Costs For Illegal Dumping of Waste." *St. Louis Post-Dispatch*, February 20, 2002, C8.

Burke, Amy. "Patriotism and Community," *Dissent* (Spring 2002), p. 45.

Camaroff, Jean, and John L. Camaroff. "Millennial Capitalism: First Thoughts on a Second Coming." *Public Culture*, 12 (2): 292.

Caplow, Theodore, and Howard Bahr. *Middletown Families: Fifty Years of Change and Continuity.* Minneapolis: University of Minnesota Press, 1982.

Chall, Jeanne. *Learning to read: The great debate.* Fort Worth: Harcourt Brace, 1996.

Chomsky, Noam. *Profit Over People: Neoliberalism and the Global Order.* New York: Seven Stories Press, 1999.

Clausen, D. *Prairie Son.* Minneapolis: Mid-List Press, 1999.

Clayton, Chris. "Family Farms Need Better Safety Net, Bradley Says." *The Omaha World Herald*, November 27, 1999, p.1.

The Columbus Dispatch. "Editorial and Comment." October 19, 1999, p. 10A.

Connelly, Deborah. *Homeless Mothers.* Minneapolis: University of Minnesota Press, 2000.

Cope, Bill, and Mary Kalantzis. *Multiliteracies: Literacy Learning and the Design of Social Futures.* London: Routledge, 2000.

Danbom, David. *Born in the Country: A History of Rural America.* Baltimore: Johns Hopkins University Press, 1995.

Davidson, Osha Gray. *Broken Heartland: The Rise of America's Rural Ghettos.* Iowa City: University of Iowa Press, 1996.

DeYoung, Alan. "Children at Risk in America's Rural Schools: Economic and Cultural Dimensions." In Rossi, R., ed., *Schools and Students at Risk: Context and Framework for Positive Change* (pp. 229-254). New York: Teachers College Press, 1994.

Douglas, Marjorie. *Eggs in the Coffee, Sheep in the Corn: My Seventeen Years as a Farm Wife.* St. Paul, Minn.: Minnesota Historical Society Press, 1994.

Draper, Norman."One third of black 11th graders have flunked state tests." *Minneapolis Tribune*, April 28, 1999, B1.

Drown, Philip. "[Prairie Town] and Surround Area/Blandin Community Investment Partnership Process Narrative, Prepared for BCIP Steering Committee." May 15, 2000. At: www.mrs.umn.edu/academic/fclt /bcipnarrative.html.

Edelman, Peter. "Reforming Welfare—Take Two."*The Nation,* February 4, 2002, 16.

Edmondson, Jacqueline, and Patrick Shannon. "Reading Education and the 21st century: Questioning the Reading Success Equation." *Peabody Journal of Education,* 73 (1999): 104-126.

Edmondson, Jacqueline. *America Reads: A Critical Policy Analysis.* Newark, Del.: International Reading Association, 2000.

———. "Taking a Broader Look: Reading Literacy Education Reform." *The Reading Teacher* 54 (2000), 6: 620-628.

———, Thorson, Greg, and Fluegel, David. "Big School Change in a Small Town," *Educational Leadership,* 57 (2000): 51–53.

Elder, Glen, and Rand Conger. *Children of the Land: Adversity and Success in Rural America.* Chicago: University of Chicago Press, 2000.

Faragher, John Mack. *Sugar Creek: Life on the Illinois Prairie.* New Haven: Yale University Press, 1986.

Fonkert, Jay. "Changing Places: Shifting Livelihoods of People and Communities in Rural Minnesota." *Perspectives.* August 2001. At: www.mnplan.state.mn.us.

Fraser, Nancy. *Justice Interruptus.* New York: Routledge, 1997.

Fredrickson, David. "Fredrickson. Rural America's Future Hinges on People Speaking Up at Capitol." *"Prairie Town" Tribune,* March 16, 2000, 4B.

Freire, Paulo, and Donaldo Macedo. *Literacy: Reading the Word and the World.* South Hadley, Mass.: Bergin and Garvey, 1987.

Freyfogle, Eric. *The New Agrarianism: Land, Culture, and the Community of Life.* Washington, D.C.: Island Press, 2001.

Foucault, Michel. *Power/knowledge: Selected Interviews and Other Writings, 1972-1977.* New York: Pantheon Press, 1980.

Fowler, Frances. "The Neoliberal Value Shift and Its Implications for Federal Education Policy Under Clinton." *Educational Administration Quarterly* 31 (1995): 38-60.

Gee, James. *An Introduction to Discourse Analysis: Theory and Method.* New York: Routledge, 1999.

———. "Reading as Situated Language: A Sociocognitive Perspective. *Journal of Adolescent and Adult Literacy* 44 (2002): 714-725.

———, Glynda Hull, and Colin Lankshear. *The New Work Order.* Boulder: Westview, 1996.

Gilroy, Paul. *Against Race.* Cambridge: Harvard University Press, 2000.

Giroux, Henry. *Teachers as Intellectuals.* Westport, Conn.: Bergin and Garvey, 1988.

———. *Pedagogy and the Politics of Hope.* Boulder: Westview Press, 1997.

———. "Rethinking Cultural Politics and the Radical Pedagogy in the Work of Antonio Gramsci. *Educational Theory* 49 (1999): 1-19.

———. *Impure Acts: The Practical Politics of Cultural Studies.* New York: Routledge, 2000.

———. "Public Pedagogy as Cultural Politics: Stuart Hall and the 'Crisis of Culture.' *Cultural Studies* 14 (2000), 2:341-360.

———. "Zero Tolerance and Mis/education: Youth and the Politics of Domestic Militarization." *Tikkun,* 16 (2001), 2:29-35.

———. *Theory and Resistance in Education:Toward a Pedagogy for the Opposition.* Westport, Conn.: Bergin & Garvey, 2001.

Gjerde, Jon. *The Minds of the West.* Chapel Hill: University of North Carolina Press, 1997.

Gordon, Greg. "Glickman Says Freedom to Farm Act Needs Fixing." *The Star Tribune*, January 11, 2000, p. 4A.

Gray, Kenneth. *Getting Real: Helping Teens Find Their Future*. Thousand Oaks, Calif.: Corwin Press, 2000.

Greider, William. "The Last Farm Crisis." *The Nation*, November 20, 2000, 11-18.

Griffith, David. "Hay Tabajo." In Donald Stull, Michael Broadway, and David Griffith, *Any Way You Cut It: Meat Processing and Small-Town America*. Lawrence: University Press of Kansas, 1995, p. 129-152.

Grimsely, Kirstin Downey. "Tyson Foods Indicted in INS probe; U.S. Says Firm Sought Illegal Immigrants." *The Washington Post*, December 20, 2001, p. A01.

Gugliotta, Guy. "Senate Passes $46 Billion Farm Bill; Fixed Payments Would Replace Crop Subsidies." *The Washington Post*, February 8, 1996, p. A1.

Gunderson, Paul. *The Houston Chronicle*, November 3, 1991.

Haas, Toni, and Paul Nachitgal. *Place Value: An Educator's Guide to Good Literature on Rural Lifeways, Environments, and Purposes of Education*. Charleston, West Va.: ERIC Clearinghouse on Rural Education and Small Schools, 1998.

Hahn, Steven and Jonathan Prude, eds., *The Countryside in the Age of Capitalist Transformation: Essays in the Social History of Rural America*. Chapel Hill: University of North Carolina Press, 1985.

Hall, Stuart. *Representation: Cultural Representations and Signifying Practices*. London: Sage, 1997.

Hanson, Victor David. *The Land Was Everything: Letters from an American Farmer*. New York: Free Press, 2000.

Hawley, David. "Distant Communities Find Common Ground." *St. Paul Pioneer Press*, February 10, 1999, C1 & C4.

Hirsch, E.D. *Cultural Literacy: What Every American Needs to Know*. New York, Vintage. 1988.

Howlett, Debbie, and Richard Benedetto. "Under Old Policy, Little Control." *USA Today*, June 4, 1997, p. 2A.

Howley, Craig, and John Eckman. *Sustainable Small Schools: A Handbook for Rural Communities*. Charleston, West Va.: Eric Clearinghouse on Rural Education and Small Schools, 1997.

Kansas City Star, Opinion, April 28, 2000, p. B6.

Keillor, Steven J. *Cooperative Commonwealth: Co-ops in Rural Minnesota 1859–1939*. St. Paul: Minnesota Historical Society Press, 2000.

Kelley, Robin D.G. *Yo mama's disfunktional*. Boston: Beacon Press, 1997.

Kellogg Foundation, *Perceptions of Rural America*. 2002. At: www.wkkf.org /pubs/FoodRur/Pub2973.pdf.

Kozol, Jonathan. *Amazing Grace*. New York: Crown, 1995.

Lane, Mary Beth. "Authorities Wary as Ohioan Takes Over Aryan Nations." *The Columbus Dispatch*, 2002, p. 1B.

Lankshear, Colin. *Changing Literacies*. Buckingham: Open University Press, 1997.

Lemann, Nicholas. *The Big Test*. New York: Farrar, Strauss, and Giroux,1999.

Lemert, Charles. *Social Things*. Boulder: Rowman & Littlefield, 1997.

Lewan, Todd, and Lewis Barclay. *Torn from the Land*. Associated Press. December 18, 2002.   At: http://www.timesunion.com/AspStories/story. asp?storyKey=72404&BCCode=TORN&newsdate=12/18/2001.

Lina, Jason. "School District in Grant-Writing Effort to Secure Funds for Long-Range Planning." *"Prairie Town" Tribune*, July 27, 1999, A1.

———. "Long-Range Planning Looks at Fundraisers, Alternatives to Them." *"Prairie Town" Sun Tribune*, December 2, 1999, p. 1 –2.

————. "Parents Say They Want Basics, Not Controversy." *The "Prairie Town" Sun Tribune*, April 17, 2002.

Lindzey, Thomas Alan. "Policies That Matter for Family Farmers." *Centre Daily Times*, May 1, 2002, p. A10.

Lyon, Larry. *The Community in Urban Society.* Prospect Heights, Ill.: Waveland, 1999.

Marcuse, Herbert. *One Dimensional Man.* Boston: Beacon, 1964.

Marshall, Ray, and Marc Tucker. *Thinking For a Living: Work, Skills, and the Future of the American Economy.* New York: Basic Books, 1992.

Martinez, Steven W. "Price and Quality of Pork and Broiler Products: What's the Role of Vertical Coordination?" *Current Issues in the Economics of Food Markets.* Washington, D.C.: Economic Research Service, U.S. Department of Agriculture, February 2000.

Mele, Christopher. *Selling the Lower East Side: Culture, Real Estate, and Resistance in New York City.* Minneapolis: University of Minnesota Press, 2000.

Meersman, Tom. "The Minnesota River in Crisis." *The Star Tribune*, December 12, 1999, p. 1R.

Memmi, Albert. *Racism.* Minneapolis: University of Minnesota Press, 2000.

McClanahan, E. Thomas. "What Promise?" *The Kansas City Star*, June 4, 1996, p. B6.

McQuillan, Jeff. *The Literacy Crisis.* Portsmouth, N.H.: Heinemann, 1998.

Michel, Lou. "Unwelcome Guests: The Hate Group Aryan Nations Plans to Set Up Its New Headquarters in Ulysses, PA, a Two-Hour Drive from Buffalo, and Residents Aren't Happy About Their New Neighbors," *The Buffalo News*, January 31, 2002, A1.

Molnar, Alex. *Giving Kids the Business: The Commercialization of America's Schools.* Boulder: Westview Press, 1995.

Morgan, Wendy. *Critical Literacy in the Classroom: The Art of the Possible.* New York: Routledge, 1997.

Morrison, Liz. "Because of Government Infusion: Farm Financials Stable in [...] County." *"Prairie Town" Tribune*, March 16, 2000.

Mouffe, Chantal. "Radical Democracy or Liberal Democracy." In David Trend, ed., *Radical Democracy.* New York: Routledge, 1996, pp. 19-26.

Nachtigal, Paul. *Rural Education: In Search of a Better Way.* Boulder: Westview Press, 1982.

Nespor, Jan. *Tangled Up in School.* Mahwah, N.J.: Lawrence Erlbaum, 1991.

Neth, Mary. *Preserving the Family Farm: Women, Community, and the Foundations of Agribusiness in the Midwest, 1900–1940.* Baltimore: Johns Hopkins University Press, 1995.

Nygren, Judith. "Gore has Farmers on Mind, Small Producers Need Help, He Says." *The Omaha World Herald*, January 14, 2000, p. 7.

Ohanian, Susan. *One Size Fits Few.* Portsmouth, N.H.: Heinemann, 1998.

Pannu, R. "Neoliberal Project of Globalization: Prospects for Democratization of Education." *Alberta Journal of Education* 42 (1996): 87-101.

Peterson, David. "Rural/Urban Forum Yields Agreement, Obstacles." *Minneapolis Star Tribune*, March 24, 1999.

————. "Differences Still Outweigh Similarities in Last Broadcast of Rural-Urban Talks." *Minneapolis Star Tribune*, April 21, 1999.

Popkewitz, Thomas. "The Denial of Change in Educational Change: Systems of Ideas in the Construction of National Policy and Evaluation." *Educational Researcher* 29 (2000): 17-29.

Ray, Tiffany. "Recently Passed Farm Bill Draws Mixed Reactions." *The Topeka Capital Journal*, May 10, 2002.

Reich, Robert. *The Future of Success*. New York: Knopf, 2000.
Ripkin, Jeremy. *Beyond Beef: The Rise and Fall of the Cattle Culture*. New York: Plume, 1992.
Rochester, Anne. *Why Farmers Are Poor: The Agricultural Crisis in the United States*. New York: International Publishers, 1940.
Roy, Arundhati. "Shall We Leave it to the Experts?" *The Nation*, February 18, 2002.
Rutherford, Jonathan. "After Seattle." *The Review of Education, Pedagogy and Cultural Studies* 24 (2002): 13-27.
Sacks, Peter. *Standardized Minds*. New York: Perseus Books,1999.
Schlosser, Eric. "The Chain Never Stops." *Mother Jones,* July/August 2001, p. 40 – 47.
Schommer, M. "Agriculture commissioner to attend World Trade Organization ministerial." *Minnesota Department of Agriculture Press Release*, November 29, 1999. At: www.mda.state.mn.us/DOCS/PRESSREL /99releas/Nov29_01.htm.
Sehr, David. *Education for Public Democracy*. New York: SUNY Press, 1997.
Shannon, Patrick. *Reading Poverty*. Portsmouth, N.H.: Heinemann, 1998.
———. "Fattening Frogs for Snakes," In Joanne Larson, ed., *Literacy as Snake Oil: Beyond the Quick Fix*. New York: Peter Lang, 2001.
———. *Becoming political too*. Portsmouth, N.H.: Heinemann, 2001.
———, and Jacqueline Edmondson. "A Look at Educational Benchmarking in the United States," *Curriculum Perspectives,*18 (1998), 3: 45–49.
Shusterman, Richard. "France's Philosophe Impolitique." *The Nation*, May 3, 1999.
Simon, Roger, Claudia Eppert, Mark Clamen, and Laura Beres. "Witness as Study: The Difficult Inheritance of Testimony." *The Review of Education/Pedagogy/Cultural Studies* 22 (2001), 285-322.
Skiba, Katherine. "Kind is at Center of Farm Dispute; He Seeks More Funds for Conservation, Not Commodity Subsidies." *Milwaukee Journal Sentinal,* October 3, 2001, p. 3A.
Smith, Marshall, and Brent Scoll. "The Clinton Human Capital Agenda" *Teachers College Record,* 96 (1995): 389-404.
Smith, Rogers. *Civic Ideals: Conflicting Visions of Citizenship in U.S. History*. New Haven: Yale University Press, 1997.
Sokol, Jason. "Solidarity on the Farm." *The Nation*, September 26, 2000, p. 6.
Spears, Tom. "Why Canada is Becoming a Nation of Pigs: Exploding Growth in Factory Hog Farms Sets Farmers Against Neighbours Who are Worried About Pollution." *The Ottawa Citizen*, March 27, 2002, p. A1.
———. "Pig Farm Neighbours Win Property Tax Cuts: Ontario, Alberta Rule Factory Farms Damage Value of Surrounding Land." *The Ottawa Citizen*, March 28, 2002, p. A5.
Stalker, Sandra. "Passing the Test: Challenges and Opportunities in Rural Schools." *Perspectives.* August 2001. At: www.mnplan.state.mn.us.
Sternberg, B. "What's the Future of Farming in Minnesota?" *The Star Tribune,* September 26, 1999.
Steyn, Mark. "Sorry Mr. Bush, you've lost your biggest fan. Mark Steyn says George Bush's steel tariffs are grave treachery." *Sunday Telegraph* (London), March 10, 2002, p. 22.
Stille, Alexander. "Slow Food." *The Nation*, August 20, 2001.
Street, Brian. *Social Literacies*. London: Longman, 1995.
Stock, Catherine McNichol. *Rural Radicals*. New York: Beacon Press, 1996.
Stull, Donald, Michael Broadway, and David Griffith. *Any Way You Cut It: Meat Processing and Small Town America*. Lawrence: University of Kansas Press, 1995.

Sturdevant, Lori. "On the Road Toward a New Rural Minnesota," *Minneapolis Star Tribune*, November 21, 1999, A23.

Sun News Services, "Bush Plants $190B Farm Bill," *The Edmonton Sun*, May 14, 2002, p. 46.

Szeman, Imre. "Introduction: Learning to learn from Seattle." *The Review of Education, Pedagogy, and Cultural Studies* 24 (2002), 1-2: 1–12.

Tabor, Mary. "Poultry Plant Fire Churns Emotions Over Job Both Hated and Appreciated." *The New York Times*, September 6, 1991, p. A17.

Taylor, Denny. *Beginning to Read and the Spin Doctors of Science.* Urbana, Ill.: NCTE, 1998.

Theobald, Paul. *Call School: Rural Education in the Midwest to 1918.* Carbondale, IL: Southern Illinois University Press, 1995.

Theobald, Paul. *Teaching the Commons.* Boulder: Westview Press, 1997.

Thorson, Greg, and Jacqueline Edmondson. *Making Difficult Times Worse: The Impact of Per Pupil Funding Formulas on Rural Minnesota Schools.* Mankato, Minn.: Center for Rural Policy and Development, 1999.

Thorson, Greg, and Nicholas Maxwell. "Small Schools Under Siege: Evidence of Resource Inequality in Minnesota Schools." Mankato, Minn.: Center for Rural Policy and Development, 2001.

Tonnies, Ferdinand. "The Concept of Gemeinschaft," In W.J. Cahnman and R. Herberle, eds., *Ferdinand Tonnies on Sociology: Pure, Applied and Empirical. Selected Writings,* Chicago: University of Chicago Press, 1925.

U.S. Department of Agriculture. *Agricultural Income and Finance: Situation and Outlook Report.* Washington, D.C.: U.S. Government Printing Office, December 1999.

Weiner, Tim. "Congress Agrees to $7.1 Billion in Farm Aid." *The New York Times*, April 14, 2000, p. A20.

Wellstone, Paul. "A 'Free Market' for Milk Pricing Would wipe Out Our Dairy Industry." *The Star Tribune*, November 29, 1999, p. 13A.

———. Keynote address for Minnesota Association for Rural Telecommunications Annual Managers' Meeting, December 9, 1999. At: http://www.senate.gov/~wellstone/On_the_Record/Speeches_Articles/martspch.htm.

Whitman, Christine Todd. "Keep the Momentum for Superfund Cleanups." *New York Times*, July 18, 2002, p. 21.

Wilson, William Julius. *The Bridge Over the Racial Divide.* Berkeley: University of California Press, 1999.

Yeoman, Barry. "Hispanic Diaspora," *Mother Jones*, July/August 2000.

Young, Iris. "The Complexities of Coalition." *Dissent* (1997): 64-69.

Index

About the Author

Jacqueline Edmondson is assistant professor of education, language and literacy education at Pennsylvania State University, University Park, Pennsylvania. Her research interests include the cultural and political aspects of literacy, particularly policy analysis and policy issues, rural literacies, and the relationship between literacy and democracy. Her work has been published by the *Journal of Research in Rural Education, Reading Research Quarterly*, the International Reading Association, *Language Arts, The Peabody Journal of Education*, and *The Reading Teacher*.